STRATEGIC INTELLIGENCE

STRATEGIC
INTELLIGENCE

FOR AMERICAN
WORLD POLICY

BY SHERMAN KENT

PRINCETON, NEW JERSEY

PRINCETON UNIVERSITY PRESS

1949

30275

JF
1525
.I6
K4
c.1

PRINTED IN THE UNITED STATES OF AMERICA BY
THE CORNWALL PRESS, INC., CORNWALL, N. Y.

TO MY FRIENDS AND COLLEAGUES OF THE RESEARCH AND
ANALYSIS BRANCH OF OSS

TO THE EUROPE-AFRICA DIVISION
AND ESPECIALLY TO THE OLD AFRICANS
R.A.W., C.J.B., H.C.M., R.P.S., J.L.H., JR., R.G.M., H.L.R.,
G.C., W.C., W.B.K., W.C., S.P.K., D.C., D.S.
— R.C., A.H.R., L.S.W. AFRICANS HONORARY —

PREFACE

THIS is a book about intelligence—not the intelligence that psychologists try to measure in a given human mind—but the kind a strategist must have to lay his plans and carry them out. Intelligence, as I am writing of it, is the knowledge which our highly placed civilians and military men must have to safeguard the national welfare.

Although there is a good deal of understandable mystery about it, Intelligence is a simple and self-evident thing. As an activity it is the pursuit of a certain kind of knowledge; as a phenomenon it is the resultant knowledge. In a small way it is what we all do every day. When a housewife decides to increase her inventory, when a doctor diagnoses an ailment—when almost anyone decides upon a course of action—he usually does some preliminary intelligence work. Sometimes the work is so informal and instinctive that he does not recognize it as intelligence—like finding the right garage man in the classified section of a telephone book. Sometimes it is formal and arduous and systematic as, for example, Arthur Koehler's brilliant analysis of the ladder in the Lindbergh case. But no matter whether done instinctively or with skillful conscious mental effort intelligence work is in essence nothing more than the search for the single best answer.

As I will be discussing it in this book strategic intelligence is an extension of this search for useful knowledge. The extension is, however, an extension in several directions. To begin with, the knowledge which strategic intelligence must produce deserves a more forbidding adjective than "useful." You should call it the knowledge *vital for national survival,* and as such it takes on somberness and stature. Then there is about it an extension in subtlety, for some of the problems having to do with national survival involve long-range speculations on the strength and

vii

intentions of other states, involve estimates of their probable responses to acts which we ourselves plan to initiate. These problems cannot be dealt with except by the special techniques of the expert. This extension in expertise is considerable. Again in the search for the subtle knowledge, difficult barriers often stand in the way. They are put there on purpose by other nations, and circumventing them calls for methods not generally familiar to the average person. In these methods lies a third sort of extension, one that leads out in the realm of clandestine investigations. (Be it said that this phase of intelligence work—the most dramatic—is pretty generally overemphasized in the lay mind.)

The last extension is one in the dimension of size. The knowledge which strategic intelligence must produce is very great in mere bulk, so large that in wartime tens of thousands of skilled people could barely make good on the job. In peacetime the task is commensurately great. This means that the intelligence process becomes one of group—as opposed to individual—effort; that there must be a complicated and careful division of labor; and that there consequently emerge problems of personnel, organization, administration, and human relations which are peculiar to the nature of the enterprise, and by no means characteristic of all familiar and homely searches for truth.

Important as they are, these extensions, as I have called them, are external to the heart of the matter: intelligence work remains the simple, natural endeavor to get the sort of knowledge upon which a successful course of action can be rested. And strategic intelligence, we might call the knowledge upon which our nation's foreign relations, in war and peace, must rest. If foreign policy is the shield of the republic, as Walter Lippmann has called it, then strategic intelligence is the thing that gets the shield to the right place at the right time. It is also the thing that stands ready to guide the sword.

Never before in our peacetime history have the stakes of foreign policy been higher. This would indicate that never before was it so important that the intelligence mission be properly fulfilled. Yet standing in the way of proper fulfillment are a number of confusions which exist among those who produce intelligence, among those who use it, and among those who are its ultimate beneficiaries —the citizens. Many of these confusions arise from imprecisions which have grown up in the language of intelligence and which have found permanence in the manuals. If the pages which follow contain words new to the intelligence trade, if they seem unduly concerned with semantics, I plead, as once did John Locke, that, "It may perhaps be censured an impertinent criticism in a discourse of this nature to find fault with words and names that have obtained in the world. And yet possibly it may not be amiss to offer new ones when the old are apt to lead men into mistakes, . . ."

The plan of this book is simple. It is based upon the three separate and distinct things that intelligence devotees usually mean when they use the word. In Part I, I consider intelligence as a kind of knowledge ("What intelligence have you turned up on the situation in Colombia?"). The chapters of this part deal with its wide and varied content.

In Part II, I consider intelligence as the type of organization which produces the knowledge ("Intelligence was able to give the operating people exactly what they wanted"). The chapters here deal with organizational and administrative problems of central and departmental intelligence.

Part III considers intelligence as the activity pursued by the intelligence organization ("The intelligence [work] behind that planning must have been intense"). In these chapters I discuss what intelligence work involves and what I conceive to be the range of problems peculiar to it.

As with books of this sort, the author is under greatest obligations to friends, associates, and disputants who have contributed wittingly and unwittingly to the text. Practically all I have written here has been the subject of long discussions with the intelligence brotherhood. My general and pervasive thanks go out to my masters and colleagues in the onetime Office of Strategic Services: General Donovan, General Magruder, William L. Langer, Edward S. Mason, Rudolph Winnacker, Donald McKay, Richard Hartshorne, Arthur Robinson and many many others. Then in a special bracket should come Charlotte Bowman, John Sawyer, Robert Miner, Beverly Bowie, and Bernard Brodie who have read and reread, edited, corrected, carped, and suggested. Without their help the work of composition would have been difficult indeed. I want to thank Alfred McCormack, another of my former chiefs, for his many profound thoughts and suggestions, and Arnold Wolfers, Willmoore Kendall, Percy Corbett, and Whitney Griswold for readings of the manuscript and many kinds of advice.

To the command, the staff, and the members of the first class of the National War College, where I had the honor to serve as one of the resident civilian instructors, I owe deepest thanks. The atmosphere of the college, the many kindnesses of its officers, and the stimulating and enlightening discussions it afforded are matters I wish to record with gratitude. With no thought of ascribing to them either approval or disapproval of the contents of this book all thanks to Vice Admiral Harry W. Hill, Major General Alfred M. Gruenther, Major General Truman Landon, and Mr. George Kennan. All thanks also to Brigadier Generals Timberlake and Picher, and to Colonels Werner, Sweeney, Twitty, Wolfenbarger, Hertford, and Moore, and to Captains Evenson and Wellings.

Most of the work of composition was done while on a fellowship granted me by the John Simon Guggenheim

Memorial Foundation. Like all Guggenheim Fellows, I want to chronicle my thanks to that institution, my deep appreciation of its generous and far seeing founders, and its kindly and efficient secretary general, Dr. Henry A. Moe.

I wish to thank George S. Pettee for any unconscious or otherwise unacknowledged borrowings from his book, *The Future of American Secret Intelligence* (Washington, D.C. 1946) which was a trail breaker in the literature of strategic intelligence. Although I find myself at variance with many of his views, all intelligence devotees, myself included, owe him gratitude for the promptness with which he formulated his own wartime experiences and put them into print.

I want to thank my university, Yale, and my department, History, for continuing my leave-of-absence status another whole academic year and thus making possible the concentrated effort which went into the work at hand.

Lastly my thanks to the Director of the Princeton University Press, Datus Smith, for his interest in the project and his wise counsel.

Quotations from Walter Lippmann's *Public Opinion* are given with the kind permission of the publisher, the Macmillan Company.

S.K.

Department of History
Yale University
October 1, 1948

CONTENTS

PART I
INTELLIGENCE IS KNOWLEDGE

CHAPTER 1

INTELLIGENCE IS KNOWLEDGE

INTELLIGENCE means knowledge. If it cannot be stretched to mean all knowledge, at least it means an amazing bulk and assortment of knowledge. This book deals with only a fraction of the total, but probably the most important fraction. It deals with the part, known to the intelligence trade as "high-level foreign positive intelligence." This phrase is short for the kind of knowledge our state must possess regarding other states in order to assure itself that its cause will not suffer nor its undertakings fail because its statesmen and soldiers plan and act in ignorance. This is the knowledge upon which we base our high-level national policy toward the other states of the world.

Notice what is being excluded. First, all knowledge of our own domestic scene is being left out. Foreign positive intelligence is truly "foreign" in purpose, scope, and substance. It is not concerned with what goes on in the United States or in its territories and possessions. Second, all knowledge of the sort which lies behind the police function is excluded. The word "positive" comes into the phrase to denote that the intelligence in question is not so-called "counter-intelligence" and counter-espionage nor any other sort of intelligence designed to uncover domestically-produced traitors or imported foreign agents. The words "high-level" are there to exclude what is called "operational" intelligence, tactical intelligence, and the intelligence of small military formations in battle known as combat intelligence. What is left is the knowledge indispensable to our welfare and security. It is both the constructive knowledge with which we can work toward peace and freedom throughout the world, and the knowledge necessary to the defense of our country and its ideals. Some of this knowledge may be acquired through clandestine

3

means, but the bulk of it must be had through unromantic open-and-above-board observation and research.[1]

It should be borne in mind—in anticipation of later chapters of this book which deal with intelligence as a process—that the intelligence activity consists basically of two sorts of operation. I have called them the *surveillance operation*, by which I mean the many ways by which the contemporary world is put under close and systematic observation, and the *research operation*. By the latter I mean the attempts to establish meaningful patterns out of what was observed in the past and attempts to get meaning out of what appears to be going on now. The two operations are virtually inseparable, though for administrative and other reasons they are often physically separated. In actual practice there are generally two different staffs each of which cultivates the respective specialisms of surveillance and research. But however far apart they get on the administrative diagram or in the development of their own techniques they are closely bound together by their common devotion to the production of knowledge.

How describe this kind of knowledge? There are at least two ways. One way is to treat high-level foreign positive intelligence as the substance of humanity and nature—abroad. This involves an almost endless listing of the components of humanity and nature. The listings can be alphabetical or topical. Whichever, it runs to hundreds of pages and would ill serve the interests of the readers of this sort of book.

The other way, and the one I have adopted, is neither alphabetical nor topical. It might be called functional. It starts from the premise that our state, in order to survive in a world of competing states, must have two sorts of state policy. The one is its own self-initiated, positive,

---

[1] Appendix I, offers a brief discussion of all types of intelligence; separates them out from each other in two rather formidable charts, and endeavors to show the interrelationship between the key types.

outgoing policy, undertaken in the interests of a better world order and a higher degree of national prosperity. The other is its defensive-protective policy necessarily undertaken to counter those policies of other states which are inimical to our national aspirations. This second kind of policy might better be called our policy for national security. I make this artificial distinction, between positive and security policies, for purposes of the present analysis.

Consider our positive policy first. To be effective, its framers, planners, and implementers must be able to select the proper instrumentality of suasion from a long list of possibles. Will it be a resolution in the UN, will it be diplomacy, will it be political and economic inducement or threat, will it be propaganda or information, will it be force, will it be a combination of several? The framers, planners, and implementers must also know where, how, and when to apply the instrumentality of their choice. Now neither the selecting nor the applying can be done without reference to the party of the second part. Before the policy leaders do either they would be well advised to know:

> *how* the other country is going to receive the policy in question and what it is prepared to use to counter it;
>
> *what* the other country lacks in the way of countering force (i.e.) its specific vulnerabilities;
>
> *what* it is doing to array its protective force; and
>
> *what* it is doing, or indeed can do, to mend its specific vulnerabilities.

Thus our policy leaders find themselves in need of a great deal of knowledge about foreign countries. They need knowledge which is complete, which is accurate, which is delivered on time, and which is capable of serving as a basis for action. To put their positive policy into effect they should first and foremost know about other

5

countries as objective entities. For example, they must know about:

a. the physiques of these countries, that is, their natural topography and environment and the multiform permanent structures which man has added to the landscape (his cities, his agricultural and industrial enterprises, his transportation facilities, and so on);
b. their people—how many; how they are settled; how occupied;
c. the status of the arts, sciences, and technologies of these people (and I would include in this the status of their armed forces);
d. the character of their political systems, their economies, their social groupings, their codes of morality, and the dynamic interrelations which prevail among all these.

Armed with this knowledge the leaders of positive policy may go forward assured at least that, if they fail, their failure will not be chargeable to their ignorance.

Secondly, consider our other sort of policy, that is, our policy concerned with the maintenance of the national security. In the interests of security our policy leaders must make constant provision for the positive policies of *other* states. Some of these policies we will have to regard as hostile to our interests and we must take steps to block them. Some, we may wish to meet half way. To frame and operate this kind of security policy we must have a second large class of information about foreign countries, and again the knowledge must be complete, accurate, timely, and capable of serving as a basis for action. We must know the nature and weight of the instrumentalities which these other countries can summon in behalf of their own policies, and we must know the direction those policies are likely to take. We must know this not only so that

6

we will not be taken by surprise, but also so that we will be in a position of defensive or offensive readiness when the policy is launched. When you know such things you know a good deal about the other country's *strategic statture,* to borrow a phrase I will develop in Chapter 4. And on the theory that there is a relationship between what a country adopts as an objective and what it thinks it can expect to accomplish, knowledge of strategic stature constitutes, in some degree at least, knowledge of the other country's probable intentions.

From the foregoing it can be seen that my first class of information to be acquired is essentially descriptive and reportorial. It is descriptive of the relatively changeless things like terrain, hydrography, and climate. It is descriptive of the changeable but no less permanent things like population. It is descriptive, too, of the more transient man-made phenomena such as governmental or economic structures. With this kind of knowledge our leaders can draft the guide lines of our positive policy, of our peacetime and wartime strategy.

The second class of information to be acquired deals with the future and its possibilities and probabilities: how another country may shape its internal forces to service its foreign policy or strategy; how it may try to use these strengths against us, when, where, and with what effectiveness. Where the first was descriptive, this is speculative and evaluative.

Within these classes of things to be known, then, we may perceive the statics, the dynamics, and the potentials of other countries; we will perceive the established things, the presently going-on things, and probable things of the future. Taken together these make up the subject matter of what I have called high-level foreign positive intelligence, or as I shall call it henceforth—strategic intelligence. Incidentally, they also indicate the three main forms in which strategic intelligence is turned out by intelligence

7

organizations. These forms are: the *basic descriptive form,* the *current reportorial form,* and the *speculative-evaluative form.*[2] Each of these is covered in a succeeding chapter.

In these coming chapters I will give a picture of the diversity and the size of strategic intelligence's substantive content. There is no gainsaying that it is both extremely diversified and extremely large. But this does not argue that the strategic intelligence business is either continuously occupied with every subject in the huge overall content or exclusively responsible for gathering all the data which make up the content. I wish to be clear about these two points.

Intelligence must be equipped to deal with the array of subjects which I will consider, and in the course of the years it may conceivably deal with all of the subjects at least once. It will, however, tend to deal with any single subject only when that subject is part of a threat to our national interest or is required by a prospective course of

[2] Here is the first place where I will depart from some of the accepted usages of the intelligence language. I take this departure, as I have noted in the preface, because of the large confusion one encounters in the lexicon of the trade. In the trade, what I have called the basic descriptive form is variously called basic research, fundamental research, basic data, monographic data, etc. What I call the current reportorial form goes by such names as current intelligence, current evaluations, current appreciations, reports, cable material, hot intelligence, etc. What I call the speculative-evaluative form is known as estimates, strategic estimates, evaluations, staff intelligence, capabilities intelligence, and so on.

On the theory that the consumers of intelligence are interested in things of the past, present, and future, I have adopted the element of time as the element of overruling importance. This permits an easy and consistent arrangement of the subject matter of intelligence and permits one to postpone cataloguing this subject matter according to use-to-be-served, consumer, etc. until a later and more appropriate stage. Few intelligence devotees have done this in the past. Far too many of them in making up their categories of the kinds of intelligence have deferred to several factors of discrimination in the same list. Thus you may find important directives of the intelligence brotherhood which contain a list of the kinds of intelligence looking something like this: (1) Basic research, (2) Strategic intelligence, (3) Technical intelligence, (4) Counter intelligence, (5) Tactical intelligence, (6) Capabilities and estimates intelligence. Such categories are by no means mutually exclusive nor are they consistent with one another.

8

action. One of the most continuously vexing problems in the administration of intelligence is deciding which particular subjects shall be watched, reported upon, or made the object of descriptive or speculative research. Equally vexing is deciding the order of their priority. The point is that intelligence is always fully occupied, but occupied almost exclusively on a relatively few subjects of real national concern. At the same time intelligence must be ready to handle a large number of subjects.

Collecting the materials necessary to handle this large number is a task which intelligence does not do solo. Intelligence shares the task with a number of institutions—both public and private. Let me confine myself to the public ones.

Although the policy, planning, and operating officers of the federal government (both civilian and military) are the primary users (or consumers) of the finished intelligence product, they themselves are often important gatherers and producers. As men who work in the world of affairs they turn out, as by-products of their main jobs, large amounts of material which is the subject matter of strategic intelligence. The best case in point is the foreign service officer in a foreign post. His main job is representing the United States' interest in that country, but a very important by-product of his work is the informational cable, dispatch, or report which he sends in. Not merely the informational cable but the co-called "operational" cable as well. For in his capacity as U.S. representative he must know much before he takes a stand, and he must explain much to his superiors at home when he has taken such a stand or when he asks their advice. Although the primary purpose of such communications is operational, they are frequently almost indistinguishable from those which flatly state the day's new developments. And thus the foreign service officer, although not specially trained as an intelligence man, is by virtue of his location and talent often a valuable and effective purveyor of intelligence.[3]

There are others in public life, such as members of special commissions, U.S. delegates to international conferences, traveling Congressmen; and that such people make significant contributions to the total task of intelligence must be borne in mind in the following chapters. Nor should the involuntary contributors outside of public life be forgotten: the writers, the newspapermen, the scholars, the businessmen, the travelers and big game hunters, even foreign governments themselves (in their official reports and releases) render invaluable aid. I would have no reader get the idea that intelligence—in shirt sleeves and unassisted, so-to-speak—is obliged to produce from scratch the prodigious body of data that it must have at hand. To make this point, however, in no way derogates the extremely important part of the total which intelligence itself does produce on its own hook. Some of this is confirmatory, and necessarily so; some is supplementary or complementary of that which is in; some is brand new and sufficient unto itself. Some is not merely new and vital, but is the stuff which would not, indeed could not, be turned up by any agency other than intelligence itself. All of it, plus the time and skill intelligence organizations employ in its appraisal, analysis, and tabulation, makes up the substantive content of our special category of knowledge.

[3] For certain key parts of the world the Foreign Service does acknowledge the need for special training, and the officers which it sends to these areas may accordingly be considered intelligence officers in one sense of the word. Most of even these however will have many non-intelligence duties.

CHAPTER 2

SUBSTANTIVE CONTENT: (1) THE BASIC DESCRIPTIVE ELEMENT

THE descriptive element of strategic intelligence is basic to the other two which I shall discuss. It is the groundwork which gives meaning to day-to-day change and the groundwork without which speculation into the future is likely to be meaningless.

The basic descriptive element deals with, or must be prepared to deal with, many things. In the succeeding pages I shall touch upon enough of them to warrant my use of the word "many." I shall draw my examples from the strategies of both war and peace, but if they seem weighted on the side of war it is because wartime has in the past offered richer experience in intelligence and an experience which may be discussed more freely than current international business.

In the recent war most of the belligerents compiled encyclopedias on countries they were contending with or which they planned to occupy or otherwise swing into their orbits. These encyclopedias should be conceived of either as a large file of knowledge in folders in a filing cabinet or in some sort of finished book form. Intelligence agencies all over the world kept this kind of file and wrote this kind of study. The British called them intelligence studies, monographs; we called them strategic surveys, topographical intelligence studies, field monographs; the Germans called them summaries of military-geographical information or naval-geographical information. Their basic aim was to provide the strategic planner with enough knowledge of the country in question to make his over-all calculations on its attributes as a zone of combat. Actually they served a hundred other uses, by no means all of which

11

were military in the narrow sense of the word. A survey of the table of contents of a typical German book will indicate the scope, if not the depth, of the knowledge required for military purposes.

I. GENERAL BACKGROUND. Location. Frontiers. Area. History. Governmental and Administrative Structure.

II. CHARACTER OF THE COUNTRY. Surface Forms. Soils. Ground Cover. Climate. Water Supply.

III. PEOPLE. Nationalities, language, attitudes. Population distribution. Settlement. Health. Structure of society.

IV. ECONOMIC. Agriculture. Industry. Trade and Commerce. Mining. Fisheries.

V. TRANSPORTATION. Railroads. Roads. Ports. Airfields. Inland Waterways.

VI. MILITARY GEOGRAPHY. [Detailed regional breakdown].

VII. MILITARY ESTABLISHMENT IN BEING. Army: Order of Battle, Fixed Defenses, Military Installations, Supply. Navy: Order of Battle, The Fleet, Naval Shore Installations, Naval Air, Supply. Air: Order of Battle, Military Aircraft, Air Installations (see List of Airdromes, etc. Special Appendix), Lighter than air, Supply.

VIII. SPECIAL APPENDIXES. Biographical data on key figures of the government. Local geographical terminology. Description of rivers, lakes, canals. List and specifications of electric power plants. Description of roads. List of airdromes and most important landing grounds. List of main telephone and telegraph lines. Money, weights, and measures. Beaches [as for amphibious military operations].

A table of contents is the bare bones of the matter; it does not reveal the character and bulk of the surrounding tissue. Consider, for an appreciation of the detail in a handbook of this sort, the kind of knowledge which lies behind some of the simple one-word entries.

Take the chapter on "people" for instance. Here one finds the latest population estimates—breakdowns according to age, sex, consumer groups, regional distribution, and so on. When you reflect that few states of the world spend the effort on their vital statistics that our census people spend on ours, and that even relatively reliable figures for these states emerge only upon large labor, you discern the importance and perhaps the magnitude of the population and manpower division of strategic intelligence. Here in the study in question one also finds sections on social structure and social attitudes, with analyses of the groupings of society—ethnic groupings, minority groupings, religious groupings, clubs, lodges, secret societies, etc., and how these groups and their members feel about God, education, filial piety, bodily cleanliness, capitalism, love, honor, and the stranger. Here are the sections on public welfare, education, and the media of public opinion.

Take the chapter on "transportation" and consider the details presented with each transportation system. The road section begins with a map of the road net; then follows a kilometer-by-kilometer log of the main routes, with observations on surface, width, grades, curves, fills, cuts, and bridges; then follows an overall appreciation of the route under survey. All these seemingly endless data have been assembled to permit the top planner and his transportation man to make the following calculation: What is the highest permissible speed which the largest and heaviest vehicle may maintain over the road from A to B and how many such vehicles may pass over the road at the speed before the road (and in consequence the vehicles) will start disintegrating?

Similarly with the railroads. Here again the gauge, number of tracks, and the routings (in the plane) are portrayed in general and detailed maps; what might be called the vertical dimension of the route is given in a profile. A well designed profile provides more than the data on grades, however; it can be (and frequently is) a kind of mile-by-mile strip-map which indicates tunnels, bridges, water points, ash pits, sidings, terminals, wyes, and repair shops. With maps and profiles are a welter of other data: subgrade, ballast, tie characteristics, rail weights and lengths, rail fastenings, signaling systems, and clearances; also an inventory by types of locomotives and rolling stock. By the time such materials are put together the planner has the data to calculate capacity of the railroad, what he should fetch along in the way of supplementary motive power and cars if he is to use the railroad, and what his maintenance problems are likely to be. If he has not these data, strategic intelligence has failed.

With ports there is another range of data: area of protected water, depth of the water (at low water ordinary spring tides), dockage and depth of water at dockside, cranes on the docks, means of transportation for clearing the docks and for clearing the harbor area, warehousing and storage facilities, harbor craft, local stevedoring situation, bunkerage and watering apparatus, and repair facilities. All these and many more things—all of them in considerable detail—you must know before you can plan the effective use of the port which you plan to capture undamaged and put to your own use. Most of these things you can find out about; some are not learned because no one asked the right question, others are almost impossible to find out about or are beyond the realm of the strategic intelligence responsibility.

14

For example, the transportation officer responsible for the debarkation of our men and equipment in the port of Algiers immediately after the assault was well supplied with the most detailed knowledge of that port, but intelligence failed him in at least two respects. It did not tell him that virtually every square yard of dock space was jam-packed with enormous barrels of wine and equally large and unhandy bales of straw. Before he could unload his own stuff he had to make way for it. This was a case of the unforeseen contingency.

The other failure is harder to excuse. One of the transportation officer's duties was to see that a number of fighter aircraft were unloaded and moved to the nearby Maison Blanche airdrome in the shortest time possible. If he could have been sure that fully assembled planes of this type could be off-loaded and wheeled down the docks, clear of the harbor area and down the highway, he would have loaded them on shipdeck ready to fly. But he was not sure of the width of the streets along his possible itineraries and so he removed the wings. If intelligence had anticipated such a requirement, or if it had been informed of it, the officer might have had his answer and thus have saved himself some time, for at least one of the routes proved amply wide for the job.

Consider the chapter on the military establishment in being. Granted that the force in being is seldom an accurate index of the war-making potential,[1] there is some virtue in knowing what exists as a nucleus of military power and the chapter in question endeavors to describe just this. It describes the components of the standing force. In broad strokes, the most important of these components on the physical side are: the number of men under arms; their allocation among the three military services—ground forces, air forces, and naval forces; their tactical and ad-

[1] This will be discussed in Chapter 4 on the speculative-evaluative aspects of intelligence.

15

ministrative organization; the quality and quantity of their equipment, large and small, the inventory of weapons according to type and performance, the fixed defenses, inventory of aircraft and warships according to type and performance; the nature of military installations—arsenals, airfields, repair depots, shipyards, etc.; and the nature of their supply, auxiliary, and medical services. On the nonphysical side there are other broad components: methods and standards of recruitment; methods and extent of training; experience under arms and experience in combat; quantity and quality of officers; quality of staff work; the identity of the important officers; the nature and force of the military tradition; the degree of esteem in which the nation holds its armed services—all of these things head up into two intangibles: military skill and morale. If my strokes were made only a little less broad this enumeration would be many times its present length.

For example, consider one small item in the above line-up of major factors—the operational airfield. There are many categories of things which must be known of it. First it must be analyzed from the point of view of how a potential enemy might use it and how well it would serve his purposes: what is its exact location on the map and its location with respect to other airfields and supply centers; what is its elevation above sea level; what supply facilities does it enjoy (its place in the transport and communications net, in the electric power grid, the character of its shops and hangars, barracks, its fuel and lubricant storage installations, its munitions storage facilities), what kind of planes can it accommodate and how many (length and type of runways and taxiways, revetments, hard-stands, dispersal areas), what hazards to air navigation does it possess (climate, weather, mountains and other natural obstacles, power lines), what in the way of protecting AA positions and smoke installations does it have?

Second, this same field might be analyzed from the point

of view of its susceptibility to attack. In this case many of the characteristics noted above are still applicable; there are also some new ones. Chief of these are: what are its identifying characteristics as seen from the air, what amount and kind of camouflage is used or may be anticipated, what is the physical vulnerability of its man-made components and their recuperability if subjected to aerial bombardment.

Thirdly, it might be analyzed from the point of view of its use to the captor if captured. This analysis would demand a number of still further data on the detailed inventory of equipment. Can the machine shops, if taken unscathed, be used for the repair of one's own planes? Can the revetments and hard-stands? If not, how much must they be modified, etc? When knowledge has been assembled to answer these questions, and many others, with respect to all the military airfields of the country, then this fragment of the chapter on the military establishment is done. Questions of the sort applicable to an airfield are roughly applicable to all other installations or major pieces of armament—naval bases, arsenals, warships—and again the knowledge brought together to answer them is a part of the content of strategic intelligence.

Let the above suffice to indicate the scope, depth, and character of a compilation of knowledge to serve one aspect of war-making. Before going over to the encyclopedias of peacetime strategy, I would like to indicate the substantive character of three other aspects of wartime strategic intelligence of the descriptive category: the intelligence of strategic air bombardment, of political and economic warfare, and of military government.

1. Strategic Bombardment

The crux of strategic bombardment (provided you have an airforce that can reach the target and bombardiers who

17

can hit it) is target selection. Assuming urgency in the time dimension, you must try to select those sectors of the enemy's war machine whose destruction will most significantly, rapidly, and permanently weaken his front line striking power. Since there may be several such sectors, and since they all cannot be destroyed in a single raid (even with the A-bomb) you must not only identify such targets, but you must arrange them in rank order of importance. The business of identifying targets and systems of targets, in terms of what their loss would mean to enemy war power, and the business of setting the priorities of their destruction, belongs properly in a later chapter, where I deal with the speculative-evaluative aspects of strategic intelligence. But both before and after this all-important evaluating operation, there are two others which partake very heavily of the descriptive.

The targets which you are after constitute, in essence, the vulnerable areas of the enemy's way of making war and maintaining a functioning society; and these most vulnerable areas cannot be picked out from the least (or less) vulnerable areas until a great deal is known about the enemy's *entire* way of life and his *entire* way of making war. Thus, whereas the strategic bombardment planner's encyclopedia need not include in detail all of the things necessary for the ground force (such as strategic geography and public health), it overlaps that encyclopedia in some places and goes beyond it in still others.

For the bombardment of a Germany or a Japan it had to describe the national economies as if the description were designed for the use of Funk and Speer or of Ishibashi and Fugiwara; it had to range out into the pattern of social institutions as if to serve Himmler and Goebbels or Konoye and Tojo. Before the planes went off on their first mission of systematic destruction, the planners for the bombardment of Germany had to know a very great deal about the airframe, aircraft-engine and aircraft-component

18

production, the production of ball bearings, of synthetic rubber, and of oil.[2] Moreover, before they decided that these sectors of the economy were the ones whose destruction would give them the most significant, rapid, and permanent weakening of German war-making capacity they had to know a very great deal about other sectors. The decision to send the B-29's against Japanese aircraft, aircraft engines, arsenals, electronics plants, oil refineries, and ultimately against the concentrations of urban population had behind it a similar stock of encyclopedic knowledge.

Once the strategic vulnerabilities were tagged and the priorities of attack settled, more descriptive knowledge was required to carry out the attack. Our bombers were to bomb physical man-made structures that the enemy was trying hard to conceal from ken, camera, and eyesight. Determination of their pinpoint location, their susceptibility to high explosive and incendiary, the ease with which they could be repaired, and so on, was more descriptive knowledge for which strategic intelligence was partly responsible. I say partly, because another part of the job was that of operational intelligence.

2. Political and Economic Warfare

Warfare is not always conventional; in fact, a great deal of war, remote and proximate, has been fought with weapons of an unconventional sort. These weapons I should like to term political and economic, and the kind of war they are employed in, political warfare and economic warfare. In both of these non-conventional warfares you try to do the two things: weaken the enemy's will and capacity to resist, and strengthen your own and your friends' will and capacity to win. Political warfare might be de-

---

[2] See the U.S. Strategic Bombing Survey (European War), *Overall Report* and *Summary Report*. (Washington, G.P.O., September 30, 1945); and the U.S. Strategic Bombing Survey (Pacific War), *Summary Report*. (Washington, G.P.O., July 1, 1946).

fined as an attempt to accomplish these ends by any means at your disposal except (1) the economic means (which I am reserving) and (2) orthodox military operations. Economic warfare may be similarly defined with the appropriate reversal of terms. In their politer guises both of these warfares have their peacetime uses; both are employed as instrumentalities of the grand strategy of peace; and both have their own intelligence requirements in war and peace.

If the reader will pause to reflect briefly on the meaning of my definition of these two warfares in their rugged and their polite aspects, he will realize that they encompass a very wide range of possible activities directed at a very wide range of objectives. Consider some of these. On the political side we may start with international alliances or friendships to be strengthened or strained and international animosities to be smoothed over or aggravated.

Within a given national state there is a wide range of potential targets: first of all the armed forces and their morale problem. Then there are the political dissidents, maladjusted social groups, the under-privileged, self-conscious minorities, labor leaders, gold-star mothers, pacifists, angry housewives, emergent messiahs, gullible or corruptible officers of government, and a hundred other categories of the misinformed, displeased, annoyed, unsatisfied, and outraged elements of the population. On the economic side there are international trade relationships and international financial arrangements to be dealt with, and within the country itself soft spots in the domestic economy that may be reached by non-military means.

The instrumentalities which total war suggests in the exploitation of these targets are large in number and for the most part as thoroughly unlovely as shooting war itself. To begin at the gentle end is to begin with the instrumentality of truth itself—truth purveyed openly by radio of known origin, by newspapers in miniature form (delivered by aircraft). Such aspects of political warfare were typical of our own Office of War Information and the British Broadcasting Corporation. Then comes the distorted truth which we call open propaganda, and with which we are pleased to associate the names of Lord Haw Haw, Axis Sally, Tokyo Rose, and the Japanese artist who designed the fulsome five-color depictions of what the "Yanks" in Sidney were doing to the wives of the Australian soldiers in the field. Next down the line is what is termed black propaganda, that which purports to come from dissident elements within the enemy's own population, but which is really carried on in great secrecy from the outside. Sometimes the black propaganda is done by radio, sometimes by leaflet, by fake newspaper, by forged letter, by any and all the means occurring to perverse ingenuity.[3] The instrumentalities under discussion thus far have been, by and large, applicable to the target by remote control; there are other instruments which can be employed only by penetrating enemy lines. This group of instruments leads off with the rumor invented and passed along by word of mouth, it includes subornation of perjury, intimidation, subversion, bribery, blackmail, sabotage in all its aspects, kidnaping, booby trapping, assassination, ambush, the *franc tireur,* and the underground army. It includes the clandestine delivery of all the tools of the calling: the undercover personnel, the printing press and radio set, the poison, the explosives, the incendiary substances, and the small arms and supplies for the thugs, guerrillas, and paramilitary formations.

The instrumentalities of economic warfare are simple and almost simon-pure by comparison. In one idiom they consist of the carrot and the stick, or in Provessor Viner's inversion, the Big Stick and the Sugar Stick. Translated into a more technical idiom they involve: blockade, preclusive purchase, freezing of funds, boycott, embargo, and

[3] See Elizabeth P. MacDonald, *Undercover Girl.* (New York, 1947).

the black list on the one hand, and subsidies, loans, and bilateral trade, barter, and purchasing agreements on the other.[4]

Before calculations of risk, expenditure of effort, and probable effectiveness of attack can be made, all phases of the polity, the society, and economy must be understood, their vulnerabilities appraised, and methods of pressure selected. A political warfare as deadly as the Germans used in Europe both before and after the outbreak of armed hostilities and as the Japanese used in the putative Co-Prosperity Sphere of Greater East Asia was based upon the most painstaking and minute surveillance and research imaginable. The sureness and deftness and timeliness of their splitting off and activating this dissident group, of increasing the worry and apprehension of that, of aggravating this annoyance and that cosmic gripe, of confusing this group of officials and subverting that, of sweeping this country into their economic orbit or virtually bankrupting that one, grew out of the descriptive knowledge which their intelligence operations prepared for this use.

3. Military Government

The war over, the responsibilities of our armed forces continued in the civil affairs activities of the military government of occupied territory. The *Army-Navy Manual of Military Government and Civil Affairs*[5] which "states the principles which serve as a general guide . . . [to the exercise of] military government and control of civil affairs in territory occupied by forces of the United States" lists the occupants' responsibilities in twenty-three named categories and one miscellaneous. These are: "Political and Administrative. Maintenance of Law and Order. Su-

---

[4] See David L. Gordon and Roydon Dangerfield, *The Hidden Weapon: The Story of Economic Warfare*. (New York, 1947).

[5] Issued by the War Department as FM 27-5 and the Navy Department as OPNAV 50 E-3, under date of December 22, 1943, p. 1.

pervision of Military and Civil Courts. Civilian Defense. Civilian Supply. Public Health and Sanitation. Censorship. Communications. Transportation. Port Duties. Public Utilities. Money and Banking. Public Finance. Commodity Control, Prices, and Rationing. Agriculture. Industry and Manufacture. Commerce and Trade. Labor. Custody and Administration of Property. Information. Disposition, or Relocation of Displaced Persons and Enemy Nationals. Education. Records. [and in case they have missed something] Miscellaneous." [6]

Of course, the degree of the occupant's responsibility within any one of the areas listed above is circumscribed by the nature of his mission—after all, he will not try to run the country at the same level of satisfaction demanded of its previous sovereign. He will try to run it with an eye merely to the prevention of those evidences of *dissatisfaction*: "disease and unrest," as the formula goes. But even so the responsibilities are large. They are so large that they cannot be undertaken without a very careful evaluation of objectives, without a very careful formulation of policy, and without a great deal of highly detailed planning. Here is another legitimate demand upon the descriptive element of intelligence, for it is impossible for the man invested with the occupant's responsibilities so much as to nibble at their edges until he knows the nature of the society, polity, and economy with which he must deal. Intelligence supplies him new encyclopedias—this time they must cover new aspects of familiar ground. When they deal with government they cannot deal with it as something to be subverted by political warfare. When they deal with physical plant it is not as something to be bombed. They must deal with those characteristics of both government and industry which the occupant must conserve for his own use. When they deal with a railroad they cannot repeat the data necessary to blow it up or the

[6] *ibid.*, pp. iv, v.

data necessary to run one's own military trains over it; they must deal with such things as its indigenous management and must furnish the knowledge to indicate how it may be put back on its feet.

In the foregoing pages I have endeavored to touch upon certain kinds of omnibus study, the first examples of which serve in the main the strategic requirements of war, and the last examples of which shade off into post-war. Before leaving the subject, however, I should mention two more kinds of encyclopedia which are typical of peacemaking and peace itself. The first can be called the peace handbook, the second the general purpose survey.

At the end of World War I, the British delegation to negotiate the peace came to Paris equipped with any number of little blue books. Sponsored by the Foreign Office and used by the delegates, they were what might be called a peacemaker's *Baedeker*.[7] In short, terse paragraphs, and appendixes containing the most important documents of state, treaties, etc., they aimed to supply the minimal needs of the officials charged with drafting the treaties. A brief of the table of contents for the two volumes on Austria-Hungary will indicate the general substance of the work.

The study is first broken down according to seven regional components of the former Austro-Hungarian Empire: 1. Austria-Hungary. 2. Bohemia and Moravia. 3. Slovakia. 4. Austrian Silesia. 5. Bukovina. Transylvania and the Banat. 7. Hungarian Ruthenia. Within each of the regional sections there is a more or less constant breakdown according to subject. The section on Bohemia and Moravia ran to 109 standard-size pages. No one who read them could possibly have remained in ignorance of the main ethnic and economic problems which were to beset the men responsible for drawing the western frontiers

---

[7] [Great Britain] Foreign Office, Historical Section; *Peace Handbooks.* (London, H. M. Stationery Office, 1920).

of the new Czechoslovakia, and no one who read them would fail to acquit himself better at the peace table.

There were many other handbooks in the series, and each emphasized those phenomena of a given country which were certain to come up in the discussions. For example, the book on France has a long and detailed section on Alsace-Lorraine; the one on Germany has sections on Silesia, the Kiel Canal and Heliogoland, and the Colonies; the one on Turkey, an excellent treatment of the Straits question; and there is one entire short study on the Yugoslav Movement.

Could there be such a thing as a general-purpose handbook of peacetime—a handbook which will contain the knowledge for peace and the knowledge necessary to meet aggression with dynamic defense? The answer is an obvious Yes. Such a handbook would be very similar to some of the encyclopedias already described. Paying for such a program of general-purpose handbooks is another matter, especially so in terms of an economy-minded Congress. Perhaps such a program could be framed within the government where the dimensions of the substantive requirements are known and then farmed out to our learned institutions which in last analysis constitute one of our most priceless strategic resources.

So far I have confined myself to the form of the basic descriptive element of strategic intelligence which is broadest in one dimension and at the same time likely to be shallow in the other. In a sense, the strategic survey of war or handbook for peacetime should be conceived of as an introductory instrument, the sort of study a man goes to when he is new to a subject. There are at least two other forms besides the encyclopedia which are worthy of mention: they are the narrow and deep study, and the thing called "spot information." Since many of the examples of the past pages were taken from a war context, these next will be taken from a peacetime context.

25

The Narrow—Deep Study

The national peacetime objectives of this country are numerous and the grand strategy to attain them a many-faceted affair. In searching for examples of the kind of narrow and profound descriptive intelligence to sustain this strategy one is virtually overcome with the multitude of possibilities. Everywhere one looks in the world a national objective is on the block. In the *New York Times* for a day taken at random [8] there were between fifty and sixty news items of concern (varying degrees of concern, to be sure) to a great many officials of our federal government. The items in this day's *Times* touched fourteen separate sovereign states, three dependent areas, five areas under U.S. occupation, and five subjects of importance all the way across the UN board. Somebody in the government —who presumably received the news over his own communications before he read it in the *Times*—had to initiate action, continue action, or change the course of the action he was already taking. It is assumed that this news landed in Washington against a solidly informed backdrop. If Washington were prepared to deal with the issues in question, what must it have possessed in the way of complete, applicable, and accurate knowledge?

Under Secretary of State Will Clayton, appeared, according to this news item, before the House Foreign Relations Committee to explain and defend a request for 350 million dollars for continuing UNRRA functions under a new policy. One of the beneficiaries of the relief fund would be China. Mr. Clayton emphasized that the distribution of relief would be rigidly supervised and controlled by the United States as benefactor. It may be assumed that in making his presentation to the Committee Mr. Clayton knew that there were people starving in China; knew that the situation was antithetical to certain of our objectives

[8] The day was 26 February 1947.

and interests, and that it was in our power to do something in defense of these objectives and interests.

An important policy decision involving quantities of the national treasure should be based upon the sort of detailed and precise knowledge characteristic of the descriptive element of intelligence. If this is the case, what kinds of knowledge on what subjects should Mr. Clayton have had?

First and foremost he should know how many people there were in China. He should know this so that when he knew the second thing, i.e., how many of them were starving, he would have his own notion of the size of the calamity. Were 2 per cent starving or were 15 per cent? Next he should know if the starvation of x per cent of the Chinese population was something that happened every year, or if it was something which was happening now because of special post-war conditions. That is, he should know how China's normal or potential food-producing apparatus equated with the requirements of the population. He would have to know this in order to decide the basic question—is there any use in our trying to feed the Chinese? For if the local food deficit were chronic and the Chinese chronically unable to produce enough food and to amass foreign exchange necessary to import sufficient foreign food, was there any point in our taking China on as a permanent charge? If this were the case and a healthy, unified, and democratic China one of our national objectives, should we not perhaps go about it in another way?

But assuming that Mr. Clayton's knowledge assured him that the situation was special, not chronic, what other things should he know? He should know how much food of what kinds would be necessary to alleviate the situation. He should know how food was normally distributed in China and if these distribution systems were partially to blame for the famine. If they were, he should know how their faults could be overcome with respect to the food he proposed to send to China, and whether or not the task of improving them would in itself be too large to underwrite. He should also know what kinds of food were acceptable to the Chinese. Even seriously undernourished people are astonishingly choosey about the staples of their diet, as was proved after the last war. He should know—in the event the Chinese insisted upon rice—if the world rice market was able to deliver the rice in exchange for dollars and the things dollars can buy. He should know, in so far as such things can be known, what internal and what international political consequences would follow a successful feeding operation on our part.

To take up the position of relief in China one can imagine Mr. Clayton armed with a study which answered all these questions and many more. It would be essentially descriptive. It would also require a large amount of work on the part of an intelligence staff, for knowledge of the kind required will not be lying around in neat bundles ready for the plucking. As to the benefits we might expect from tiding China over a rough spot, the discernment of these is a task of appraisal and evaluation and is the subject of another chapter.

Spot Intelligence

The last category of strategic intelligence—descriptive—is what the trade calls "spot intelligence," or "Information Please," or "Ask Mr. Foster." The kind of knowledge which it supplies is usually in answer to some innocent-sounding question like: What side of the road do cars run on in Petsamo? What is the best map of southern Arabia? What is the depth of water (LWOST) alongside the Jetée Transversale of Casablanca? Where is U Saw now? What are the characteristics of electrical current at the commercial outlets in Sidney? How much copper came out of the Bor mines in 1937? How good is the water supply in Hong Kong? When did Lombardo-Toledano last go to

Venezuela? What are the administrative units of the USSR? And so on.

With this sort of question, the answer to which is usually cast in words, there are other questions which are answerable only by the map, the diagram or plan, and the photograph. The descriptive element of strategic intelligence must stock such items or know where to find them.

In some cases such questions have a strategic importance, in many they do not. On the other hand it can be argued that if an organization can answer all such questions, it has on file the knowledge to answer more important ones. Distasteful as the "Ask Mr. Foster" function is to strategic intelligence, it is probably a legitimate one and the substantive content an important fragment of the store of its total knowledge.

From the above it can be seen that in order for us "to assure ourselves that our cause will not suffer nor our policies fail because they are ill-informed" our intelligence organizations must be prepared to describe a large number of phenomena. They must be prepared for more than this however. For description involves a stopping of the clock of time and the real clock cannot actually be stopped. It goes on, and descriptions of the things of yesterday are out of date tomorrow. To remedy the defects inherent in a necessary but artificial stopping of the clock, a second element of intelligence is essential. This is the current reportorial element which aims at keeping certain descriptions up to date.

CHAPTER 3

SUBSTANTIVE CONTENT: (2) THE CURRENT REPORTORIAL ELEMENT

THE pages immediately preceding have dealt with a knowledge of things and people as they were at a given moment of time. The phenomena of life which appear in the formal encyclopedias can be regarded as frozen in mid-passage. Such an accumulation of data as has been described would be virtually all strategic intelligence required were it not for the element of motion in human events. The obvious fact, however, is that practically nothing known to man stands completely still, and that the most important characteristic of man's struggle for existence is the fact of change. Knowledge devised to fit the requirements of grand strategy must everlastingly take into account this fact of change. Keeping track of the modalities of change is the function of strategic intelligence in its "current reporting" phase.

Before embarking upon an analysis of the areas of human activity in which change occurs and where intelligence should note the changes, it is worth making the point that the streets through which change moves are many-way streets, and there are many kinds of change. For example, it is as important to know that the standing military establishment of a potential enemy power is being demobilized as it is to know that it is being built up or merely reoriented around a new weapon or a new tactical concept. It is as important to know that the level of prosperity in a friendly country is rising as it is to know that it is going on the rocks. It is as important to know of the emergence of a friendly government in a hitherto hostile state as it is to know of the overthrow of a friendly government in a hitherto friendly state. In fact the direction of change is sometimes more important to know about than the absolutes of quantity, extent, effect, etc. Thus this matter of direction, without falling strictly into the area of content, is one of highest significance.

If the current reportorial phase of intelligence is to do the job, in what specific areas of human activity must it observe and report change? Or, put another way, if one very important part of the intelligence mission is the observation of day-by-day developments (surveillance) what phenomena should be put under surveillance? There are two ways to approach the answer to this question. One would be to list areas according to their known or foreseeable priority of interest to the grand strategy of this country. If this method were adopted the first area for the U.S. in A.D. 1949 would necessarily be either that of a foreign power's program of atomic research, biological and chemical warfare instruments, or in the successes and failures of the international Communist movement. The second area might be changes in the armed establishments of the world, or in the economic well-being of the world, or in the political stability of the world, or in its moral fervor to do right. It would take a wise man to set these priorities, and it is my feeling that the resultant listing would have neither the cheering element of certainty nor the comforting quality of logic.

The second way to approach such an analysis of content would be according to some established and logical pattern of humanity and human activity—would be to fall back upon the time-worn rubrics which social scientists have used for decades. This method has the advantage of logical order, but it runs the risk of submerging important matters in a welter of unimportant ones. But since the object of this chapter was to lay out the substance of one element of strategic intelligence and was not to serve as an exhortation to operating intelligence agencies of the moment, I will adopt this latter method and follow its formal subdivisions.

1. *Personalities.* On the theory that the *basic-descriptive* element will have chronicled in its biographical files and posted in its biographical encyclopedias the names of people who were important as of a certain date in the past, the reportorial element must keep track of the goings and comings and liaisons of these people. More important even, it must in addition pry beneath the surface of past leadership to discover the emergent figures of tomorrow. Who knows the name of the British Prime Minister or the leader of the French Communist Party in 1960? Who knows the head of the Soviet Union in 1955? Who will be the chief of staff of the Yugoslav air force? Who will be the leaders of a divided Palestine? Who will be president of Lever Brothers or United Chemical? Who will be the director of the Pavlov Institute and leader of the Latin American Confederation of Labor? The men who will hold these jobs some day are alive at this moment. Where are they? What are they doing? What sort of people are they? The future is by no means entirely free to nominate such officials by random choice. The chances are that the future will be obliged to make its selection from a fairly narrow slate of candidates. These candidates are at this moment the comers in business, in the military, in the trade union movement, in politics, the arts (let us not forget Paderewski), education, and the conspiratorial underground. The job is to find out about these emergent leaders and to watch their progress upward, so that as revolutions brew and violent or natural deaths approach, the possible human replacements for the ousted or dead will be well known.

Since every man is both the product and molder of his environment, and since no two men are exactly alike, an intelligence operation to do its reportorial job on men must know a great deal about them. It must know of their character and ambitions, their opinions, their weaknesses, the influences which they can exert, and the influences before which they are frail. It must know of their friends and relatives, and the political, economic, and social milieu in which they move. Only by knowing such matters can the emergent character be invested with the dimensions of leadership, and only by knowing such matters can one guess at the sort of change toward which the new leader will strive when he comes to power.

2. *Geographic.* On the theory that there are already descriptions of what I have earlier called the physiques of other countries, the devotees of current reporting must be continuously improving and extending these descriptions. Not merely must they chronicle the new changes that man is making upon the landscape—many of which appear in section 4 below, but also they should be abreast of the widening of the horizons of geophysical knowledge. What new facts are being learned or can be observed in such matters as erosion rates, the silting of rivers and harbors, weather, beaches, water power sites and supplies of drinking water. What is being discovered or can be noted in the fields of hydrography, geodesy, and geology.

3. *Military.* Again on the assumption that the armed force-in-being, as outlined in the preceding chapter, has been carefully described as of a certain date, the reportorial element has the task of keeping track of developments within the establishment. It must know of new legislation which will set the size and quality of the force for the year or years to come. It must keep track of recruitment policies and their success and failure. It must keep track of changes in the training of the enlisted man and the officer. It must know developments in the indoctrination of troops, the social strata from which the corps of officers is recruited, the economic status of men and officers. No matter what the difficulties, it must try to keep track of those changes which the other country properly regards as

33

its own military secrets: such things as new fighting ships, new types of aircraft, new weapons of all horrendous sorts, new devices for improving fighting efficiency,[1] changes in morale and in the loyalty of the force to its government in its regional, its political, its religious, and its nationalistic orientation.

4. *Economic.* Again on the theory that the handbooks have stopped the economic machine at a certain point in time and described it, the reportorial element has the task of keeping track of current economic developments. It must note the emergence of new economic doctrines and theories—for purposes of example I cite the range which lies between Keynesian theory, down through Ham and Eggs, to the Technocrats. It must keep careful track of changes in the housekeeping side of the armed forces, administrative reorganizations and the like, and it must note changes in government economic policy—policy affecting industry, the organization of business, agriculture, banking and finance, and foreign trade. It must know the changes which are occurring in the size and distribution of national wealth and income, of changes in the standard of living, wages, and employment. It must watch for new crops and the developments of new methods of agriculture, changes in farm machinery, land use, fertilizers, reclamation projects, and so on. It must follow the discovery of new industrial processes, the emergence of new industries, and the sinking of new mines. It must follow the development of new utilities and the extensions of those already established. It must follow changes in the techniques and implements of distribution, new transport routes and changes in the in-

---

[1] It is hard to say, and perhaps footless to try to decide whether such matters as non-fouling marine paint, atabrine, radar, the use of blood plasma, and any number of similar matters belong under the military or some other heading. Perhaps the decision as to their appropriate allocation should be made according to the degree of secrecy with which their sponsors hold them. Plainly it seems that highly classified things like espionage and counter-espionage, belong here.

ventory of the units of transportation (autos and trucks, locomotives and cars, transport aircraft, canal boats, and blue water merchant shipping). Perhaps most importantly in the age of atomic fission, it must note discoveries in new natural resources, notably at the moment the discovery of high-grade uranium deposits.

5. *Political.* The reportorial element must pay strictest attention to changes of a basic constitutional nature and events such as those which have recently occurred in France and Italy, and which may soon happen elsewhere in the world. It must observe how political power units are lining up on significant issues, and how such units may be splitting up into factions, disintegrating into other groups, or joining them *en bloc.* It must watch changes in the basic political doctrine of these groups. It must take note of changes in relationship among the central, the regional, and the local political authorities, and the major shifts in policy toward domestic, foreign, colonial, and imperial problems. It must follow new legislation which will affect political expression, to make it either more free or less free. It must watch national and local election results and the emergent political figures mentioned earlier. It must follow the course of new pressure groups and other types of organizations which are capable of political influence from outside of party framework. It must know of new governmental and administrative techniques.

6. *Social.* Perhaps the most important single social phenomenon that the reporting element must watch is that of population. It must watch it in all its aspects: its growth or decline, and its rates of growth and decline; changes in its age groups, its occupational groups, and consumer groups. It must watch for changes in its distribution between city and country, between region and region. It must take note of migrations within the country and emigration from the country, and until time and permanent residence envelops them, it must have an eagle eye out to

displaced persons. There will also be changes in the social structure which are closely allied to certain phases of economic change, and which must come under constant observation. What groups are emerging to social and economic eminence, what groups or classes of groups are sinking? What are the developments within that particular element of population known as the labor force? The reportorial element of intelligence must keep track of its changes in size and structure, and above all must watch how it is organizing, and under what leadership, for its struggle with management.

What is happening to church membership, who is joining clubs and what kind of clubs are they, who is founding new lodges, secret societies, and cooperatives? Intelligence, in this aspect, must also know a large number of other things about the society, such as changes in the way of living, development of new housing, changes in the home economy and family diversions. It must be aware of changes in taste, manners, and fashions. It must follow the program of educational institutions of all levels, and worry almost as much about the changing content of the elementary history textbooks as it must about changes in the curricula of the highest graduate and professional schools. It must concern itself with government policy toward education at all levels and with changes in the relationship between government on the one hand and non-governmental organizations, such as the churches, the trade unions, the clubs and societies, on the other. It must know of the changing relationship among minority groups within cultural, social, and economic groups, and it must watch for the changes in the statutory and judge-made law, which in turn change the course of human behavior throughout the population pyramid.

7. *Moral.* Within the wide range of matters moral the reportorial element must heed changes in the basic doctrines of life: the waxing or waning or religiosity, of pa-

triotism and nationalism, of belief and confidence in the regnant order and in the national myths. It must know of the change in popular attitudes toward the purge of undesirables, the nationalization of private property, party government, civil marriage, lay education, rights of minorities, universal military training, to hit a few of the high spots.

8. *Scientific-Technological.* Since much of the world to be will be the product of science and technology, the reportorial element must watch these with sharpness. It must know of any developments that might be of significance for foreign policy considerations in mathematics, physics, chemistry, zoology, geography, oceanography, climatology and astronomy. It must know what is happening in the realm of the social sciences. What are the students of sociology, economics, psychology, geography, law, and history, and so on coming up with? What new ideas are they getting that will some day have the influence of the discoveries of a Locke, a Rousseau, a Darwin, a Pavlov, a Freud, or a Haushofer? What is happening in the medical schools and the clinics; what are the new diagnoses, the new remedies, the new treatments? What is going on in the realm of telecommunications: the telephone, the telegraph, the submarine cable, and above all, radio? What is happening in the world of cartography? What new areas of the world and phenomena of life are being charted on the map? What new purposes are old theories being applied to, what new uses for old materials? How are any or all of these being applied to armaments?

The preceding paragraphs cover a staggeringly large area of continuing human activities. I have written them thus in an endeavor to portray the dimensions of subject matter and not as an exhortation to the reporters of the surveillance force to keep every square inch of it under active and systematic observation. It should be thought of as describing most of the real and many of the potential responsibilities of the reporting function. The question which at once arises is what fragments of the enormous whole are actually to be put and kept under scrutiny. There is no categorical answer. The only answer is one to be put in the form of a differential—namely: only such fragments as are positively germane to national problems which are up now and other problems which appear to be coming. Those should be dealt with first which are matters of established national importance. They will vary from country to country and from time to time.

For instance, what is going on in the French General Confederation of Labor, in the Politburo, in Zionism, in the Peron government, in the Philippine cabinet, in the uranium mines of Joachimstal, Czechoslovakia, in the Pasteur Institute, is of greater national significance than the extension of the Ouagadougou Railway, the new budget of Mexico, or the changing literacy rate in China. However, this is not to argue that matters which in the short term are as relatively unimportant as the last example may not some day in some circumstances deserve first priority treatment. Nor is it to argue that all matters of first or even second degree importance are to be identified by some simple rule of common sense such as the "national interest" rule I have given. Perhaps the greatest difficulty which the surveillance force must face in carrying out the reportorial function is not so much the amassing of knowledge on present and foreseeable problems as in looking out into the future and in trying to identify matters which will one day themselves become problems.

As the reporting element carries out its task it constantly adds freshness to the content of the basic descriptive element. It does more than this, for in keeping otherwise static knowledge up-to-date it maintains a bridge between the descriptive and what I have called the speculative-evaluative elements—a bridge between the past and the future.

CHAPTER 4

SUBSTANTIVE CONTENT: (3) THE SPECULATIVE-EVALUATIVE ELEMENT

To INTRODUCE this most important and most complicated element of strategic intelligence a few fairly obvious facts are worth a brief restatement.

The world with which the United States must do business is very largely composed of separate sovereign states, and the kind of business the United States must do ranges through all the possible stages between most pacific and most belligerent. By many and diverse means we try to promote a better world order. We undertake and make good on collective agreements reached in the UN; we undertake and make good on bilateral and multilateral agreements with other states and groups of states; we exert pressures of many sorts in behalf of world well-being and our own security; and we go to war. In carrying out this vast amount of enormously complicated business we must be foresighted. We should be prepared for the future; we should put every effort into being well-girded for its contingencies; we must not be caught off balance by an unexpected happening. In the perfect grand strategy nothing that happens can have been unexpected.

The problem of this chapter is the analysis of what the United States must know in order to be foresighted—what it must know about the future stature of other separate sovereign states, the courses of action they are likely to initiate themselves, and the courses of action they are likely to take up in response to some outside stimulus. The knowledge which is at issue is far more speculative than that discussed in the last two chapters, viz., the basic descriptive, and the current reportorial. The obtaining of it puts a very high premium on the seeker's power of evaluation and reasoned extrapolation, and that is why I have called it the speculative-evaluative element of strategic intelligence.

What knowledge should the U.S. have about the future of other states in order to have the requisite foresight?

Let me first create a hypothetical state, Great Frusina, to use in giving the answer to this and subsequent questions.

About Great Frusina the United States should know two things. These are: (1) What is Great Frusina's *strategic stature*, (2) what *specific vulnerabilities* does Great Frusina possess which qualify her strategic stature? As I hope to demonstrate, if the United States can answer these two questions, it will be in a fair way to answer the next. This one is: What *courses of action* will Great Frusina be likely (a) to *initiate herself*, and (b) to *take up in response* to courses of action initiated elsewhere. To produce answers for all these questions is difficult, but that is not the problem here. The problem here is to put the finger on the kinds of things we must know and the method we must employ before we begin to produce the answers. The problem is to identify the kinds of knowledge which are at once the solid runway from which our speculations must take off and the compass which must guide them in flight. Identification of such knowledge cannot proceed until at least two of the terms of recent coinage (strategic stature and specific vulnerability) are given a bit more precision and definition.

Strategic Stature [1]

By *strategic stature* is meant the amount of influence Great Frusina can exert in an international situation in

---

[1] One of my critics has objected mildly to my use of the word stature. As something of a purist he correctly points out that it does not

which the United States has a grand strategic interest. This is a broad statement, and not broad by inadvertence. For instance, by *international situation* I mean any of the differences of opinion, misunderstandings, disputes—minor and major—which may occur between sovereign states and which have a remote or immediate bearing upon world security. I mean any of the dislocations in the relations between states of the world which by their nature must have an adverse effect upon Great Frusina's security and material welfare. Given the oneness of the contemporary world there will be few situations which Great Frusina can neglect as unrelated to her security and welfare and a great many in which she will therefore exert some sort of influence. By *influence* I mean influence through any of the instrumentalities that states employ in peacetime or wartime—influence through moral suasion, propaganda, political and economic threats, inducements, and actual penalties; through acts of reprisal (in the non-technical sense); threats of hostility, and war itself. Strategic stature is thus the sum total of sugar sticks and big sticks which Great Frusina possesses, to which must be added her willingness to use them and her adeptness in using them.

To get at strategic stature there are a number of things you must know, and the first of these is the probable "objective situation" [2] in which Great Frusina may be ex-

---

quite comport with the dynamic role I have assigned to it, that it is a word more closely allied to stasis than action. My reply is that contemporary usage permits such an expression as "the stature of British diplomats," by which is meant something more than their height, girth, and weight. Diplomatic stature includes the tact, persuasiveness, ingenuity, and wisdom as these are manifested at the conference table or elsewhere. Stature in this sense is the latent power which entrance into the diplomatic ring will make dynamic.

[2] By "objective situation" I mean the situation as it exists in the understanding of some hypothetical omniscient Being. I mean the situation stripped of the subjective characteristics with which a prejudiced human observer is almost certain to endow it. I use the word "probable," because, whereas knowledge of the *objective situation* is of highest desira-

pected to exert influence or throw weight. There are at least two elements in any objective situation which are likely to be ever-present; they are the element of geographical location and the element of time. There are other elements which are likely to differ from one situation to another. To cite at random a few for purposes of illustration is to list such intangibles as the degree of real or fancied gravity involved in the situation and the Great Frusinan nation's popular appreciation of the gravity; the degree of the nation's acceptance of the sacrifices it must make to liquidate the situation; the power line-up, that is, what friends can Great Frusina count on for support in the situation and how much support, what friends can Great Frusina's opponent count on for support?

The constant and variable elements in the situation which are hinted at above are often of overriding importance. That is, the geographical position of the contestants, time, the power line-up may rule, and the situation be liquidated in terms of them.[3] But many situations arise in which these elements do not rule and in these latter instances there are two more extremely important things you must know before you can begin to gauge Great Frusina's strategic stature.

The first of these is the weight, applicability, and effectiveness of Great Frusina's *non-military instrumentalities* of policy and strategy. The second is what people have called Great Frusina's *war potential*. Let us take them up one at a time.

---

bility, any non-omniscient Being (i.e. any frail human being) *probably* can never apprehend the true objective fact. He should, however, strive until it hurts.

[3] For example, if the government of Liberia became outraged at the government of Paraguay (or vice versa) for any given reason, one could assume that the state of outrage would pass without much having been done about it. In the years not so long back, when the sovereign components of the world were less tightly knit and the projection of power by even the greatest states was a slower and more cumbersome process than it is today, similar self-liquidating situations were more common.

By Great Frusina's *non-military instrumentalities* are meant the range of levers, short of the great lever of military operations, which lies between such a simple thing as a properly worded and properly delivered formal note of objection or invitation, and such a complicated and dangerous thing as an embargo, blockade, or other stringent kind of economic sanction. Also are meant such things as our telling Cuba that we dared not continue shipment of thereapeutic narcotics to her as long as she afforded haven to Mr. Lucky Luciano—a man well known to us as a dope peddler and general bad egg, whom one of our states had been at great expense to catch, indict, convict, jail, and later deport back to Italy. We did not want Mr. Luciano in our backyard and we used a mild non-military instrumentality to get him out of it.

The Soviet's use of the Comintern and now the Cominform, the paraphernalia of party infiltration and front organizations, state trading, and even the World Federation of Trade Unions offer corresponding cases in point. Great Frusina will have such levers to push, such strings to pull, and such needles and ice-picks to manipulate. Knowledge of them and their weight, applicability, and effectiveness constitutes part of the knowledge necessary to estimate her strategic stature in a given situation the objective facts of which are already discernible.

By *war potential* is meant the possible power to make war. To be somewhat artificial, it may be useful in talking of war potential to distinguish between Great Frusina's actual *military force in being* and her *mobilizable military force*. This distinction is artificial because much of the force in being is itself not completely and uniformly mobilized; it is not fully prepared to get up and go at a moment's notice.[4] It must be topped off, so to speak, and

---

[4] Our garrison troops on the Island of Oahu were supposedly a mobilized force on the morning of the Pearl Harbor attack. Yet while the attack was going on some of these troops were in process of drawing weapons from a supply sergeant. The latter, an orderly man, was requiring

this topping off—i.e. the issuance of battle equipment, the moving up to the line of attack, the arrangements for supply and auxiliary services, etc.—is itself indistinguishable from the essential and characteristic aspects of mobilization. But even though much of the force in being needs some finishing touch, there are likely to be units which are completely mobilized and ready to start shooting. Hence the distinction.

Now the problem before us is what must intelligence organizations know with respect to the *situation,* the *non-military instrumentalities,* the *force in being,* and the *war potential* of Great Frusina so as to make an evaluation of her strategic stature in a foreseeable or given situation.

As to the *situation.* Realize that it has not yet arisen and that the first big question for intelligence is to try to imagine what it will be like when it does arise. To sharpen the imagination intelligence must have a great deal of the descriptive and reportorial knowledge discussed in previous chapters. For example, it must know a great deal about the political and economic structure of Great Frusina, about internal political and economic tensions, about her foreign relations, and the apparent grand strategic plan within which she is working. Intelligence must know a great deal about the strategic geography of all parties to the situation, and must have some sort of rational basis for calculation of the time factor. Intelligence's reportorial staff must have kept the organization fully informed of developments as they watched them clandestinely and overtly, so that the speculative take-off will be from the most extreme point on the runway and the flight of imagination aimed in what will prove to be the truest direction.

It is perhaps worth mention here that calculations on strategic stature which are not based on some sort of an-

---

each of the soldiers to sign a memorandum receipt for what he took. This is an example of what I mean by "topping off" in an extreme situation.

ticipated, imagined, or rationally assumed situation are
not likely to be meaningful. It is the context of the
situation alone which gives point and meaning to the subsequent elements of the speculation. To talk about non-
military and military instrumentalities without setting the
limits of the situation in which they are to be used, to
talk of them as if they would be the same for all situations, is to me, without much sense. There can be no
such thing as a calculable national potential—potential for
the achievement of goals by peaceful or warlike means—so
long as the calculation proceeds in a vacuum. Only when
you fix the adversary, the time, place, and the probable
means to be used can the calculation have point.

As to the non-military instrumentalities: again, knowledge of them is based on what intelligence has been able
to find out about Great Frusina's inner stability and
strength and the ways she has conducted her international
business in the past. Which of these instrumentalities she
will use and with what weight and effectiveness she will
use them, intelligence can hazard to guess only when its
knowledge of Great Frusina is comparable to that of her
own minister for foreign affairs and her own chief of state.
Intelligence may hope to possess such knowledge only as
it has studied deeply and systematically her polity, society,
economy, and the moral tempo of her people, and as it
has been able temporarily to transmute itself into the
Great Frusinan foreign minister and see the situation from
his particular perspective. This again is the kind of knowledge dealt with in the two preceding chapters. Ideally it
is coldly objective and factual, it is accurate and complete,
up to the moment.

In actual practice it is often none of these things. No
matter how hard intelligence personnel try, no matter with
what skill and insight they work, they cannot objectively
and factually describe everything the way they might
choose. Certain phenomena elude description. Maybe

they are supersecret and have been successfully concealed from sight—like the Japanese shallow-water torpedo. Maybe they are there, and always have been there, for anyone to see, photograph, measure and tabulate, but have gone unnoticed for a multitude of reasons. Take for example the little colony of Sardinian-born Italians which has existed in Tunisia; take the beaches of a number of South Pacific islands; take the possible axle-loadings and clearances on Balkan railroads. Still again, maybe they were always there and have been accurately described, but are no longer open to re-examination and the published descriptions have been lost. Faced with the necessity to provide objective and factual descriptions of such phenomena, intelligence simply cannot deliver; it inevitably falls back upon the sort of description which is a small speculation in itself. It may be an interpolation between two known and related phenomena, an extrapolation from an established base, a pure deduction, or a depiction from analogy.

As to *war potential:* First, your knowledge of the partly and wholly mobilized force in being will have been supplied by the people who report such matters. In the nature of things, the reporting people of the intelligence organization in question are the military, naval, and air attachés, sent openly to Great Frusina, who are permitted to know certain fairly large brackets of data about Great Frusina's military establishment. Great Frusina permits this in exchange for similar knowledge from the countries to which she sends her own military attachés. Characteristics of her armed forces such as their newest weapons, the techniques of their use,[5] and new tactical doctrine which Great Frusina regards as a great national resource and capable of being kept secret, she tries to keep secret. When

[5] To be a little more explicit, the U.S.S.R. is known to have a high ability in the use of rockets, but exactly how it uses this weapon is not known. That the U.S. has radar bombing equipment is generally known but the technical use of that equipment is regarded as a military secret.

these matters are discovered and reported, therefore, their discovery is often a matter for clandestine intelligence operations. As a general proposition every country knows a great deal about all other countries' forces in being and a great deal about most of their weapons. What they are likely not to know about are weapons of a highly effective nature which Great Frusina has held so closely that even her own troops have not been permitted to practice with them and learn them.[6]

To ascertain Great Frusina's mobilizable military establishment, or as it is called, war potential, is a very large order. Were it not the single most important element in Great Frusina's strategic stature and an absolute must for her opponents, the opponents would not ever attempt the calculation. But in as much as naked power, or the threat of it, is all too often the force which decides international disputes or liquidates situations such as those I am talking about, it is mandatory that we have some reasoned estimate of the amount of naked power Great Frusina can muster under given conditions.

I say that the computation which intelligence must attempt is a large order. I say this because it involves striving for an answer to the following prodigious question: What amount of active military power, or better, lethal energy, can Great Frusina dig out of herself; how many men and how well trained to fight in ground, air, and naval units armed with all the complicated weapons of modern combat can Great Frusina produce in what amounts of time; how much such force can she be prepared to project to the most strategically advantageous or necessary battleground and be prepared to maintain there?

What must intelligence know to answer such a question?

[6] The atomic bomb is of course the outstanding case in point. You would have a very difficult time in finding out even the names of the men who knew how many bombs were in existence, and an equally difficult time in naming the men who know how the bomb worked.

47

It must know a great many facts and it must know a method of combining them. It must know a very great deal about Great Frusina's actual and latent resources,[7] and it must have the will, the wisdom, and the highly technical skill to arrange its knowledge of these facts as Great Frusina's General Staff and her Office of Production Management [8] will normally have arranged them before they made their fateful decision. At no place in the intelligence operation is the professional training of the intelligence producer of more importance. The job of synthesis upon which he is embarking is one which requires of him the very highest competence in one or more of the sciences, of politics, economics, geography, and the military art. He should not undertake it unless he has an easy familiarity with the literature and techniques of the relevant disciplines.

What about Great Frusina's resources? I will take them first and I will be brief about them—not because they are unimportant—but because people who deal with mobilization and the foundations of national power deal with them endlessly. So endlessly, in fact, that one sometimes gets the impression that the matter of war potential is simply a matter of identifying quantities of men, of steel, of kilowatt hours, of machine tools, railroad lines and trucks, etc., adding up the quantities, and deriving from the resultant sum a sort of index number which is meaningful. I cannot agree with this method of computing war potential. Thus without giving the impression that you have all when you have a line-up of Great Frusina's actual resources let me name them.

[7] In my opinion the most egregious error in war-potential computation is the error of confining one's attention to resources and neglecting the country's power to combine them to get an appropriate end-product. On a straight numerical calculation of resources there is likelihood that India and China might emerge as a threat to the U.S. or U.S.S.R. No conclusion could be more useless.

[8] See U.S. Bureau of the Budget, *The United States at War* (Washington, D.C., G.P.O., 1947) for the fullest and the only official account to date of the process of our mobilization. This document is required reading for all students of war potential.

The first is her geographical location and the quality and extent of her terrain. Next is her population, quantitatively speaking, especially that part of it which lies in the age bracket 17 to 45, and qualitatively speaking, its health, vigor, and degree of general and technical education. Thirdly are the raw materials and power sources she possesses or has unequivocal access to: mineral (including uranium), forest and fishery resources, water power, etc. Fourth are food and feed stuffs; next, standing industrial plant and the means of distributing the finished product. Sixth is the transportation net and the inventory of vehicles; seventh, the political structure of the state and its stability; eighth, the social structure and the inventory of virtues which as social beings the population possesses; ninth, the moral quality of the people and the kind of values for which they are prepared to make sacrifices. Sometimes this list is shortened down to the three primal items: manpower, raw materials, capital equipment; and sometimes it is spun out, as anyone can see it might be, to fill pages and pages.

If intelligence knows the facts or approximations thereto, which are indicated in the list above, it has a part of the knowledge involved in a war potential computation. But it must also be aware of what the process of mobilization is and what it involves. Intelligence must know this before it can apply a method to the data and get a useful result. Let us say then that mobilization is in essence a matter of internal national *adjustment* or *readjustment*. A country organized for the welfare of its citizens and for its security must now put security way out in front and the citizens' welfare an appropriate distance in the rear. And a country which has never seemed to put the welfare of its citizens in front will push this consideration even farther to the rear.

This means that a certain large percentage of the most productive age group of the population—the men and women between 17 and 45—are taken out of civil life and put in uniform. Before mobilization is done, this group may be 10 per cent of the total population or even more. It also means that this group (as a group) is supported in terms of food, shelter, clothing, medical care, transportation, communications, and insurance at a higher average level than it enjoyed in civil life. Lastly it means that this group is furnished with the complicated and expensive implements of war and is taught to use them in the most effective manner. To this situation there must be adjustments. What are the adjustments? How successful is Great Frusina likely to be in making them? These two questions are the points of departure for gauging the net effectiveness of mobilization.

The adjustments in question must take place first within Great Frusina's *polity*. Even though her government may be as dictatorial as Hitler's in 1936, there still must be political loin-girding. The less concentrated the political power of peacetime, the greater must be the adjustment, for the measures Great Frusina is to take elsewhere in the rearrangement of her national life require that the executive arm of government be given almost plenary powers.

To begin the estimate of Great Frusina's capacity to mobilize, intelligence must have at hand as full a catalogue of political knowledge as may be and with this knowledge intelligence must endeavor to foresee the degree of success that the Great Frusinan statesmen may achieve in adjusting the peacetime polity to fit a condition of war.

The second and most important adjustments which the new government must now initiate and supervise are the adjustments in Great Frusina's *economy*. Before intelligence looks at specific sectors of the economy in order to find out how they are doing, there are three things about it intelligence must know. These are overall things which will influence every decision taken with respect to war

50

production and the civilian standard of living, which in effect will almost predetermine the magnitude of mobilized power which the nation can muster. These three things are (1) the amount of fat on the economy, (2) the amount of slack in the economy (this could be considered another kind of fat), and (3)the amount of flexibility of which the economy is capable.

By *fat*, I mean such things as some of the things Britain had at the start of World War II: extensive external assets, a large merchant marine, access to necessary raw materials and the credits to buy them without going into current production, a large and up-to-date supply of capital equipment, a large inventory of finished goods, a national diet of three to four thousand calories per day, etc. Important elements of German fat may be said to have existed in the excess capacity of machine tools, a large amount of brand new plant and new housing. The Italians had practically no fat, indeed little enough lean.

By *slack*, I mean such things as the 40-hour week, twelve to sixteen years of education for youth, small proportion of women in the labor force, unemployment of both labor and capital, only partial utilization of equipment, etc.

By *flexibility*, I mean the capacity of the economy to beat plowshares and pruning hooks into swords, and that in jig time. I mean the ability of the technicians to make typewriter factories over into machine gun factories, and put the manufacturers of dry breakfast food into the shell-fuse business. I mean the ability to make synthetics from scratch where the natural sources have dried up.[9] When

---

[9] As might be imagined, war-potential computers are of many types—among them is one class which is constantly trying to find a key item in the mobilization process which will serve as an index to the whole difficult process. Some of this group hope to find the answer to their prayers in the national income; that is, they are hoping to find a way of correlating national income to war potential, so that when the former is known, the latter too is known. Others feel this way about kilowatt-hours. There are several other schools. It has seemed to me that their neglect of

you have the facts to calculate the fat, slack, and flexibility of the economy you are armed with a sort of basic knowledge which makes the pursuit of further economic knowledge profitable.

Adjustments within the economy must take place along two main lines. The economy must produce a vastly increased amount of goods, many of which are munitions, and at the same time the economy must provide a tolerable standard of living for the civilian population. To accomplish these ends the economy must be pretty severely shaken. What must intelligence know to gauge the extent of the shake-up and the results?

It must know how enlargements in standing capital equipment, power resources, and in the labor force [10] are being contrived; it must know how strategically-necessary raw materials are being stockpiled, and for those in short supply, what success is attending the development of substitutes.[11] It must know how speedily and efficiently heavy

---

other general factors, particularly this factor of *flexibility of the economy* makes their conclusions peculiarly vulnerable.

[10] With respect to German mobilization for World War II, it is interesting to note that up until 1936 the Nazis had been bedeviled by unemployment and had partially mended matters by contriving the "Küchen, Kinder, Kirche" slogan for women. German women under this party exhortation went back to the kitchen and left jobs open for the men. When mobilization began (it was not known as such) in 1936 and the economy could have advantageously used a larger labor force, the Party did not dare, for political reasons, welch on the slogan and call the women back to the factories. Certain types of economist who seldom bow to anything but a straight economic consideration may mull this over with profit, for here is a case where a political commitment ruled even though there was a significant economic penalty attached. See Frank D. Graham and J. J. Scanlon, *Economic Preparation and Conduct of War under the Nazi Regime* (mimeographed report of the] Historical Division, War Department Special Staff, Washington, D.C., April 10, 1946). Cited here and elsewhere by written permission of the issuer.

[11] In preparing for World War II, the Germans had to make very extensive adjustments of this sort. Foreseeing shortages in crude oil, natural rubber, high-grade iron ore, sulphur, copper, natural fibers and a number of other items, they made advance provision. They developed processes for the production of synthetic oil, rubber, and fibers; they developed methods for utilizing their own low-grade iron deposits, and found adequate substitutes for materials they could not synthesize or

industry is being changed over from the manufacture of the machines of peace to the engines of war, and how deftly light industry is being shifted from consumer durables to shell fuses, range finders, radar components, and small arms. It must know these things—in so far as they may be known or estimated—and hundreds like them. Then it must be able to gauge how well the government is handling its share of the adjustment: how it is allocating raw materials, making its contracts with private enterprise, financing essential blocks of war industry, arranging for the equitable distribution of scarce consumer goods, and curbing inflation. It must know how tolerable the government is able to make an otherwise intolerable life to the civilians who must produce the implements of war, suffer the economic hardships of war, bear its tragedies and still be denied the incentives of active participation.

None of the things that I have mentioned above can be known in the same way that one can know the number of miles of paved street in City X or the number of sugar beet refineries in County Y. To possess the knowledge necessary to estimate economic war potential, intelligence must have far more than a checklist of capital goods, labor force, and raw materials; it must have a great deal of general wisdom about the capacity of Great Fusina to pull these resources together, the strength of its political authority, its unity and resolve, its managerial competence. The intelligence worker must have a willingness to transmute himself into the Great Frusinan who is deputed to boss the mobilization. He must realize that the issues he is facing up to are issues of the magnitude of national survival and that he may pull any trick in the book—dirty,

---

stockpile. Allied intelligence underestimated their capacity to do these things. It tended to speak of the shortages themselves as top items in the list of German specific vulnerabilities. This was not really the case. The real vulnerability lay in the pool of manpower, too large a portion of which had to be allocated to the relatively inefficient production of substitutes for the short commodities.

unorthodox, "unsound" in classical terms, and illegal—if it will get him his results.

The third major group of adjustments attendant upon mobilization and about which intelligence must know is the group of *social* adjustments. It must have knowledge of them if it is to complete its calculation of war potential. It must know how the people will adjust to the loss of luxuries, amenities, and even necessities; how they will react to poorer if not less food, less clothing, more crowded living conditions, and less civil liberty; how they will take the departure of their young people, the disruption of families and family businesses, and the grim prospect of casualties. As in the case of economic adjustments few of these things can be definitely and positively known. Intelligence must settle for approximations which emerge sometimes from devious indirect methods of inquiry. If it cannot find out by public opinion poll, for example, exactly how people are reacting to rationing, it may find indirect evidence thereof by following changes in government rationing regulations. These may be available in the newspapers and may indicate in so many words that the black market is booming or that civilian compliance is high. One cannot stress too heavily the importance of the indirect approach where the direct one is impossible, nor can one overstress the fact that the devising of the indirect approach—"formulation of the method" it would be called in formal terms—is itself an act of intelligence and an essential part of the whole intelligence process.

The last category of adjustments which the Great Frusinans must make and of which intelligence must take note are those within the code of their national *morality*, within their established values of good and bad. Here, perhaps, are some of the most difficult tasks which intelligence must face and some of the most important to solve. On the assumption that intelligence can put the finger on the accepted moral values of life in peacetime, and on the assumption that these values are not all of them values which will forward victory in war, the problem for the government is to try to alter these values or remodel them. The problem for intelligence is to tell how the pepole will react to these attempts. For example, let us suppose that the Great Frusinans were brought up on the message of Jesus, how easily will they make the transition to a war morality where all evil things are pragmatically, at least, justified? How many people are going to be pacifists or conscientious objectors, and if any large number are, how will their point of view affect the success of mobilization? Or suppose Great Frusinans, like some of the Orientals, view the business of staying alive with indifference; as soldiers do not expect to survive a war, indeed often seem to welcome, if not actually court, death, what can intelligence discern in this attitude which will qualify its overall guess on war potential? A correct estimate along these lines in re Japan, for instance, would have told us much about the long-range capabilities of its air force.

The preceding pages have been addressed to the first of two questions posed with respect to mobilization; What adjustments must Great Frusina accomplish in turning from peaceful pursuits to preparations for the use of armed power? The second question is yet to be answered. It is: How successful is she likely to be? Since we are talking primarily about knowledge of mobilization and not the process itself this question might better be put: What must you know to estimate the success of Great Frusina's effort to mobilize?

You must know with as much certainty as possible *Great Frusina's own appraisal of the situation* against which she is prepared to mobilize. How do the elements of time and space (geographical relationships) shape up in Great Frusina's probable calculations? Has she the time to prepare, and once mobilized can she expect to project her military power to a spot on the earth where it will do some good?

Secondly, you must know many of the other things mentioned earlier, especially what I have called the fat, the slack, and flexibility of the economy.

Thirdly, you must know with what skill and will Great Frusina is able to plan, coordinate, and implement the huge job of administering the mobilization.

Fourthly, you must know something of the government's probable performance with respect to the civilian economy. Will it do a good job and will the citizens realize it? Will they be able to see results commensurate with their efforts and sacrifices, or will things appear to be as bad as the gloomy ones have predicted?

When the speculative element of strategic intelligence knows these things—as a result of drawing heavily for basic data from the descriptive and reportorial elements—it is in a fair way to be able to know the dimensions of Great Frusina's strategic stature.

Specific Vulnerability

In speculations about Great Frusina's future it is not enough merely to analyze and add up her strategic assets. There are subtractions to be made before we can hope for any realistic appraisal of her future weight in the world and the courses of action she may choose to initiate or take up in response to outside stimuli. The negative quantities in question are what I am calling her *specific vulnerabilities*.

By these words I do not mean the general indefensibility of her frontiers or the destructibility of her cities, or any other such thing that may be common to a great many states and may constitute a broad strategic weakness against which a strong opponent may direct his general attack if war became inevitable. Assuming that Great Frusina is one of the world's strongest powers and that frontal attack with any of the non-military or military instruments of grand strategy is too costly to contemplate, does she possess soft spots the exploitation of which will yield results disproportionate to the outlay of effort? If she has such soft spots she has what I am calling *specific vulnerabilities.* The problem is: What must you know to know the location and nature of Great Frusina's specific vulnerabilities?

The answer to this question is that you must have the kinds of encyclopedic knowledge described in the last two chapters; [12] and from that select, by analytical processes, those facets of the life of Great Frusina which are vulnerable to the weapons you possess. The weapons, as noted earlier, are of many sorts: psychological, political, economic, and military.

During World War II we identified and misidentified a large number of specific vulnerabilities of our enemies. Unquestionably our correct identifications hastened the victory. Among the readiest examples of successful selections in the field of strategic air bombardment were the attacks on German synthetic oil production and aircraft

[12] To the over-anxious and not too responsible intelligence devotee a loud warning should be sounded at this point. In the quest for specific vulnerabilities no intelligence operation can conceivably afford to canvass the whole field of Great Frusinan culture. The discovery that all dental chairs are made in a single factory which is vulnerable to sabotage or air attack, or that ration cards are easily counterfeited, or that there is a pacifist cult tucked away in the mountains, cannot possibly warrant the time necessary to uncover such facts. On the assumption that these matters are vulnerabilities and specific enough to suit anyone, their successful exploitation by an outside power will mean no more than a trifling inconvenience to the Great Frusinan government. People will use rocking chairs at the dentist's; new ration books may or may not be issued; the pacifist cult will be liquidated at the cost of one government casualty. The quest for specific vulnerabilities must take place in areas which will be dictated by common sense and a knowledge of the limits of one's own instruments of exploitation. It should be further limited by the doctrine of comparative costs: if you can deliver a 1,000-ton cargo by air, will you make more converts with this cargo in the form of leaflets or high explosives. If the latter, you should probably slow down on your research into the weakness of civilian morale and the appropriate content of your leaflets. But, conversely, the size of the rubble pile is not necessarily the index of effectiveness.

and on the Japanese cities and the Hokkaido-Honshu coal ferries. On the other hand, attacks on certain phases of German transportation and the Japanese fleet in Kure cannot be said to have been attacks on specifically vulnerable targets. The knowledge which dictated these latter operations could have been improved.

Peacetime affords as many examples as wartime of specific vulnerabilities, and of their exploitation by the non-military instrumentalities of grand strategy. For instance, the Soviet Union's ambivalent position with respect to the western frontiers of Poland is a case in point. To the Poles, the U.S.S.R. was saying, "We assure you the Oder-Neisse line," and to the Germans in the Soviet-occupied zone whose support the Soviets were earnestly seeking, the U.S.S.R. was saying, "As agreed at Yalta, the Oder-Neisse line is not a closed issue." Mr. Byrnes in his Stuttgart speech of September 1946 used the political instrument to exploit this vulnerability to the hilt. When he asked the Russians if they had decided how this frontier would be fixed he forced them to close a decision they wished to keep open. It will be recalled that the Russians had to forsake the comfortable double position and reassure the Poles, thus losing support in Germany. This was precisely Mr. Byrnes's plan.

Other comparable examples are in the papers almost daily.

Probable Courses of Action: Estimates

I have urged that if you have knowledge of Great Frusina's strategic stature, knowledge of her specific vulnerabilities, and how she may view these, and knowledge of the stature and vulnerabilities of other states party to the situation, you are in a fair way to be able to predict her *probable courses of action.*

To strengthen the reliability of your prediction you should possess two additional packages of knowledge.

First, you should know about the courses of action which Great Frusina has followed in the past. Does the history of her foreign policy reveal a pattern which she will adhere to? Has she followed certain lines of international behavior for so long that they have hardened into traditions with proven survival value. Or are they myths founded in irrationality? Will these traditions or myths exert an influence—even though an illogical influence—upon her probable present course of action? Has Great Frusina an old friend with whom she will never break; has she had over the years a real need for an "eastern ally"; has she a traditional "life-line of empire" to maintain, or the urge for "ice-free ports"? Knowledge of this order is important, but must be used with caution. For while the force of tradition is strong, the present moment may be the very one in which Great Frusina is girding herself to break with the past.

Second: you should know, as closely as such things may be known, how Great Frusinans are estimating their own stature in the situation. Great Frusina is not herself immune to errors in judgment, and as we have seen in the cases of both Germany and Japan in World War II, is capable of misconstruing the situation, overestimating her own chances of success, and underestimating the strength of her opponents.

One may say in summary that if intelligence is armed with the various kinds of knowledge which I have discussed in this chapter, and if it commands the welter of fact which lies behind them, intelligence ought to be able to make shrewd guesses—estimates, they are generally called —as to what Great Frusina, or any other country is likely to do in any circumstance whatsoever. Note that intelligence does not claim infallibility for its prophecies. Intelligence merely holds that the answer which it gives is its most deeply and objectively based and carefully considered estimate.

In such fashion intelligence should have a reasoned opinion on what policies a country is likely to initiate within the next year of its own free will. If one should want to know, intelligence should be able to estimate the chances of nationalization of a particular British industry in the next six months and the effect such a move would have on Britain's balance of payments. Likewise intelligence should be able to estimate another country's reaction to outside stimuli. How will a country react to such stimuli as a U.S. policy, a policy of some state other than the U.S., an act of God, or natural calamity. What for instance, would be the probable reactions of the U.S.S.R. to an arrangement whereby the U.S. secured rights to the naval and air facilities of Mers el Kebir, Bizerta, Malta, Cyprus, and Alexandria? What would they be to a violent swing to the left of the British Labor Party or the emergence of Communist Party control in France?

Before leaving this subject the question should be asked: in terms of the myriad qualifications introduced all along the line, how valuable is the "knowledge" which emerges from this element of strategic intelligence? Are the so-called "estimates" of intelligence of any value? My answer is Yes, they are of very great value if they are soundly based in reliable descriptive data, reliable reporting, and proceed from careful analysis. The value may not be an absolute and ultimate one; the speculative evaluation or estimate may not be exactly accurate, but if individual lives and the national security are at stake I would prefer the indexes of strategic stature, specific vulnerability, and probable courses of action as they emerge from this phase of strategic intelligence to the indexes afforded by the only alternative, i.e. the crystal ball. In actual fact, many a speculative estimate undertaken along these lines by the experts has been astonishingly close to what actually came to pass. The social sciences have by no means yet attained the precision of the natural sciences; they may never do so. But in spite of the profound methodological problems which they face they have advanced prodigiously in the last fifty years. Taken as a block of wisdom on humanity their accomplishments are large not merely in the area of description but more importantly in the area of prognosis. If the record did not read thus, this book most emphatically would not have contained a chapter on this element of the long-range intelligence job.

A Note on Capabilities

Although this discussion has faced up to the possibility of war and the mobilization of armed power, and although I have drawn many illustrations from wartime, it has so far been cased in a context—and hope—of peace. It has been written as if we were directing our peacetime policy toward maintenance of peace and national security, but at the same time we were remembering that we might be thrust into a war which we must win. The question may be put: What happens to the speculative-evaluative element of strategic intelligence when the context is war? How are our speculations changed by the introduction of a state of war? The answer is, our speculations change in emphasis and direction, but not in any fundamental sense.

For example, the components of strategic stature are somewhat altered. To begin with, the *situation* may well be much clearer when it is upon us than when it was out in the future.[13] We are likely to be able to give a larger degree of certainty to the time factor: When may we expect the major effort? We are likely to be able to discern much

[13] However, the coming of war by no means gives us an absolute certainty about the situation. The unexpected or unanticipated happenings of the last war demonstrate this. I doubt if any strategic prophet on 1 September 1939 foresaw the date of Italy's entrance into the war, the date of Germany's attack on the U.S.S.R., the date of the Japanese attack upon Pearl Harbor, the date of Italy's surrender. On 1 September 1939 we knew more about the situation than a year earlier, but we by no means had a perfectly clear picture of how the situation was destined to change in some of its major proportions.

61

more clearly the geographical-spatial elements of the situation and foresee exactly the place or places of major and diversionary attack. The line-up of allies and enemies will in the main be much clearer though we may never be able to call the turn exactly.

Next, although the enemy is still using his non-military elements of grand strategy, they have been converted into quasi-military instruments. Political pressures and inducements are used with the gloves off and become political and psychological warfare. The economic big stick and sugar stick become the implements of economic warfare.

The armed establishment in being is now the already-mobilized fraction plus what was mobilized during the emergency period. The big question with respect to military power is now referred to as the country's *capabilities*.[14] When the military use the word "capabilities" they mean a state's ability to achieve a given objective expressed in time and force requirements. They apply the word to both themselves and the enemy. In a situation where the enemy's objective is precisely defined—viz., his objective to contain an amphibious operation (Normandy), or capture a vital strategic objective (Stalingrad), or destroy by aerial bombardment his enemy's ability to stay in the war (the first blitz of London or the V-weapon attack), or destroy his merchant marine (the Atlantic campaign), a broader and more explanatory definition is permissible. In this latter context we might say that "capabilities" means the amount of armed force (ground, naval, and air power) that the enemy can mount on a battle line or battle lines and maintain there at maximum operational activity, without undue damage to over-all strategic commitments, without

---

[14] This is a time-honored military word and I have kept it sacrosanct to use in just this place. The temptation to use it in a peacetime context as an alternative for *strategic stature* was strong. To have done so might have been a temporary favor to military readers, but the final result would have been to spoil one of the few words in the intelligence vocabulary that is still fairly pristine.

overstraining or ruining the home war economy, and without shattering the staying power of the polity and society.

The issue of mobilization is technically at least a dying or dead one for the problem of the peacetime war potential has been transmitted to the problem of *maintenance* of the armed force at the level of maximum operational activity. Nearly all the factors of war potential are still very much in the calculation which intelligence must make, but since the war is on, not in the offing, the word "potential" might well be dropped or qualified.

Specific vulnerabilities are, if anything, of intensified importance and their identification one of the major tasks of intelligence. They are being exploited with all effective and available weapons, and defended with all the skill, ruse, and strength the enemy can muster for the task.

Our side will be calculating the courses of action open to the enemy in terms of our estimate of his capabilities. Military doctrine shys away from trying to be so specific as to put the finger on the one course of action the enemy is most likely to take; it shys away from the identification of what is often called the enemy's "intentions" or "probable intentions." In an estimate of the alternative courses of action of which the enemy is capable the military formula known as the "estimate of the situation" is used. Roughly speaking, this formula runs as follows: (1) knowledge of the environment, i.e. the terrain, weather and climate, hydrography, logistics, etc., (2) knowledge of the enemy's strength and the disposition of his forces, (3) knowledge of one's own forces, (4) probable courses of action open to the enemy.[15] The courses of action will lie primarily in the field of military operations, but secondarily and scarcely less importantly in the fields of political and economic relations.

To make an estimate of *enemy capability* in wartime you

[15] In a later chapter I will discuss the "estimate of the situation" formula at greater length.

must have possession of the main categories of knowledge needed to gauge what I called the strategic stature, and specific vulnerabilities of peacetime. To get at *probable courses of action* you have to know much the same sort of thing you needed for estimating probable courses of action in peacetime.

In totting up these similarities we must not forget one very large dissimilarity. In peacetime it is not too difficult a task to come by the sort of basic knowledge you must have to make these speculations (the U.S.S.R. excepted). Before World War II you could have known a great deal about any country of the globe and now after the war you can again by no greater outlay of effort (the U.S.S.R. excepted). But during a war, when the enemy knows full well the importance of keeping you in ignorance, the getting of the basic knowledge is quite another matter. It can be had, and much of it through perfectly overt channels, but the effort necessary to get it has been multiplied many times.

Throughout this chapter the theme has been the theme of speculative knowledge. In discussing this element in the content of strategic intelligence I may have given the impression that speculative knowledge is a common commodity which is to be had for the gathering. If I have given this impression, I wish to correct it. Speculative knowledge is not common and it is not to be had for the gathering. It is the rarest ingredient in the output of intelligence and is produced only by the most competent students this country possesses. It requires of its producers that they be masters of the subject matter, impartial in the presence of new evidence, ingenious in the development of research techniques, imaginative in their hypotheses, sharp in the analysis of their own predilections or prejudices, and skillful in the presentation of their conclusions. It requires of its producers the best in professional training, the highest intellectual integrity, and a very large amount of worldly wisdom. In this case, what I am speaking of is not the important but gross substance which can be called recorded fact; it is that subtle form of knowledge which comes from a set of well-stocked and well-ordered brain cells.

PART II
INTELLIGENCE IS ORGANIZATION

CHAPTER 5

INTELLIGENCE IS ORGANIZATION

INTELLIGENCE is an institution; it is a physical organization of living people which pursues the special kind of knowledge at issue. Such an organization must be prepared to put foreign countries under surveillance and must be prepared to expound their pasts, presents, and probable futures. It must be sure that what it produces in the way of information on these countries is useful to the people who make the decisions: that is, that it is relevant to their problems, that it is complete, accurate, and timely. It follows that such an organization must have a staff of skilled experts who at the same time know (or can be told) what the current foreign policy and strategic problems are, and who will devote their professional skill to producing useful information on these problems.

In discussing organization in this chapter, I do not wish to get into its detailed administrative aspects. There are, however, certain problems of intelligence organization which I will discuss at some length in a later chapter (Chapter 8). In this section I want to confine myself to some general comments on organization and the kinds of people it must include.

Some of the staff must be particularly expert as on-the-spot observers and as such will make up the bulk of the overseas surveillance force. They are the men stationed in foreign capitals whose job consists of observing and reporting. They are the people who supply in large measure what I have called the current-reportorial element in strategic intelligence. What are the qualities of the ideal overt [1] foreign observer, information officer, or attaché?

---

[1] It goes without saying that the first quality of a *clandestine* observer is an inpenetrable cover or disguise, which at the same time does not unduly restrict his observational activities. He should have other things

To begin with, there are some superficial qualities which are none the less important. He must not dislike foreigners or living with foreigners; he must be adaptable to the conditions of life abroad; he must be something of an extrovert who is good with people. Too often men possessed of these obvious surface qualities and none of the deeper ones are chosen for foreign duty. This is poor policy, for such a man may not be much sharper as an observer than any casual American tourist or expatriate. What he must have beyond all things is a high capacity to detect the significant and a high sensitivity to changes which occur in the matters he is watching. He has acquired this sensitivity by becoming a specialist in his subject. These qualities which he has acquired by study and experience make up the screen of sensitivity he exposes to the foreign scene.

But everything that such a screen picks up will not be of concern to the home intelligence organization. Only certain things will be. To select these certain things he must possess a second screen which was made in the U.S.A. That is, he must be as thoroughly sensitized to the information requirements of his country's foreign policy and strategy as he is to the foreign scene he is observing. He must know what is wanted, what is important and unimportant.

Lastly, he must be no mere passive receiver of impressions. He must continually be asking himself embarrassing questions. He must be imaginative in his search for new sources of confirming or contradicting information, he must be critical of his new evidence, he must be patient and careful in ordering the facts which are unchallengeable, he must be objective and impartial in his selection of hypotheses—in short, although his job is not primarily a research job, he must have the qualities and command the techniques of the trained researcher.

beside cover, many of which are the same as those to be described for the overt observer.

70

Organizationwise, all this means that the intelligence service must recruit trained and gifted people, must keep them in the home office until they are thoroughly familiar with the things that this government will want to know, and must see to it that, once in the field, they are kept fully posted on changes in the government's informational requirements. The overt foreign surveillance staff is thus an overseas extension of the surveillance and research staff which remains at home. At least it ought to be. Its intimate connection with the home staff should be emphasized and formalized by rotation of assignment.

In addition to the people who are on surveillance duty abroad, the intelligence organization of course has a home establishment. The staff of this home establishment is busy on a home-based surveillance job and the research job. In the circumstance that home surveillance is an overt occupation there is a large overlap between the qualities of the surveillance and research men. In fact, the jobs of the two so completely merge that more often than not one man does both jobs all the time. At his surveillance task he leafs through the day's take of radio broadcasts, foreign press dispatches, the key newspapers from the foreign country of his specialty, cables and reports from relevant field observers and attachés. While at his research job, which he may be conducting at the same time, the data he acquires each day as he watches the daily parade of events, are likely to be important pieces of his study. If he does not keep abreast of what is happening today, his research will lose sharpness and direction—not to say completeness.

The qualities necessary for an overt surveillance man on field duty apply with equal vigor among this home surveillance and research group. These people, too, must be aware of the reigning problems of foreign policy, they must be students highly trained in the matters which make up the problems of that policy, they must have the capacity

71

for painstaking research and impartial objective analysis, Some of the work they do will be in the field of the natural sciences; most of it in the area of the so-called social sciences (in which I include the military art). The questions which they must answer are obscure and can be reached only by knowledge of out-of-the-way languages and the techniques of higher criticism developed by the scholar; often they are subtle, and subtle in a way understood only by a man who has lived with them and understands their subtleties almost by intuition.

Consider for purposes of illustration two small problems related to our landing in North Africa. Long before that operation was set, the United States through an agreement with the Vichy French government was sending to French Morocco, Algeria, and Tunisia occasional shiploads of consumer goods, including petroleum products, cotton piecegoods, sugar, and tea. All along, and especially in the summer of 1942, the potential propaganda value of these goods was well understood: if they could be properly packaged and if they could carry some sort of message bespeaking our cause so much the better. What should this message be? What languages should it be written in? How should it be phrased? The problem was in essence one well known to our advertising men, but then again it was not. They could devise a label which had a fair chance of success when applied to Americans, but the audience in question was not American, it was predominantly French and Arab. How do you reach the soul and conscience of the colonial Frenchman and of the North African Arab? You have to know as much of their psychologies, ruling ideologies, habits of thought, and manner of expressing themselves as you know of your own people.

Of the many hazards to success consider the actual phrasing of the message in Arabic. The language is an old one and at present is rapidly adapting itself to the new world its users confront. Many things have happened since the

Koran became a written text; the new concepts of democracy, totalitarianism, liberalism, and so on must be given a nomenclature before they can be expressed. Today's Arab journalists and politicos and professors are doing just that and our experts who know only the language of the Arab classics could not possibly translate the message in question. The American to do the job is the one who not only knows modern journalistic and spoken Arabic, but that particular subspecies of the green language which is written and spoken in the local centers of Northwest African Arab culture: Fez and Marrakech, Oran, Constantine and Kairouan. Unless an intelligence organization could produce such a man, either from its own resident staff or from its roster of consultants, it would fail in its obligations.

Another case in point was the problem of estimating the available local labor force an army could count on in Spanish Morocco. If the problem were given to someone expert in manpower computations but innocent of the special situation in Spanish Morocco, the answer would be grossly misleading. The expert would begin his mistaken way by taking Spanish Moroccan census figures at face value, he would compound his error by assuming that the people noted in the census could be physically reached, by assuming that incentives could be devised to get them to work, and by assuming that once employed they would be able to do the sort of work required of them. Without a Spanish Moroccan expert at the manpower man's elbow to tell him that the census was inflated, that the people were scattered in tiny communities throughout the rugged and virtually communicationless country; that the last thing such people wanted to do was work; and that if they could be induced to work the supervision problem would be enormous—in short, without a man to add the local correctives—the result would indeed be misleading. Such a man can develop the necessary competence only through

73

the method suggested. An intelligence organization must have a large number of such real experts.

These examples are not cited to suggest that we would have been defeated on the beaches of North Africa if we had not known how to write the Arabic language of French Morocco, or if we had overestimated the local labor supply of Spanish Morocco. Different examples could prove that without a large amount of comparable special knowledge, the costs of our landing would have been appreciably higher.

My point is that not just anyone can hold a professional job in an intelligence organization. My point is that an intelligence organization is a strange and wonderful collection of devoted specialists molded into a vigorous producing unit.

In a sense, intelligence organizations must be not a little like a large university faculty. They must have the people to whom research and rigorous thought are the breath of life, and they must accordingly have tolerance for the queer bird and the eccentric with a unique talent. They must guarantee a sort of academic freedom of inquiry and must fight off those who derogate such freedom by pointing to its occasional crackpot finding. They must be built around a deference to the enormous difficulties which the search for truth often involves.

Intelligence organizations must have appropriate facilities, prime among which are a library and a quiet place to work. The library must contain both published reference works and the welter of classified documents which are the news of today and the raw materials of tomorrow's analysis. The library must be well run, by which I mean, run after the fashion of the ideal of American libraries. It will, of course, not be a general library, but it will be an extensive one in the area of current happenings abroad. As to the quiet place to work, I mean something a great deal more conducive to concentrated intellectual work than the

forty odd square feet of floor space per person which prevailed during the war.

But that intelligence organizations bear a resemblance
to a university faculty is not enough. They must be geared
to a quicker pace and must be more observant of deadlines
even though this may occasionally and regrettably involve
a sacrifice in accuracy. Intelligence organizations must
also have many of the qualities of those of our greatest
metropolitan newspapers. After all, many of their duties
have a close resemblance to those of an outstanding daily.
They watch, report, summarize, and analyze. They have
their foreign correspondents and home staff. Like the
newspaper they have their privately developed hot sources;
their speedy and sure communications. They have their
responsibilities for completeness and accuracy—with commensurately greater penalties for omission and error.
They have their deadlines. They have the same huge
problem of handling the news in millions of words per
day and seeing that the right staff man gets all messages
which fall appropriately into his field. They even have the
problem of editorial control and the difficulties of reproduction and dissemination. In these terms it is fitting
that intelligence organizations put more study upon newspaper organization and borrow those phases of it which
they require.

Along with the newspaper and university aspects, intelligence organizations must have certain characteristics of
good business organization. It is by no means through an
inadvertence that the language of intelligence organizations
is weighted with words from business. Intelligence can be
thought of—indeed it often is—as an organization engaged
in the manufacture of a product (knowledge) out of raw
materials (all manner of data) and labor (highly skilled,
but not practical in the business sense of the word). The
product, to be worthy of the label, must be up to standard. It must be packaged in a multitude of ways to suit

the diversities of consumer demand. Some consumers want it in semi-finished form (field notes with comments upon them), some want it finished but in bulk (the encyclopedia), the most pernickity want it in small amounts done up in gift wrapping (the one-page summary of the world situation in words of two syllables or less). Not only in its packaging, but in its very inner make-up must the product both direct and reflect the fluctuations of consumer taste, or better, consumer requirements. Let Hungary threaten to go Communist and the Hungarian ingredient must be stepped up; let Panama ready itself to take a stand against us in the matter of bases and the Panamanian constituent will have to be increased. By using its backlog of experience it can anticipate—even create—consumer demand for a new product, but only by maintaining the quality can it expect continuous acceptance. Like many a producer of consumers' goods, intelligence will have its greatest marketing success when its product bears the unmistakable signs of superior research, cautious development, sound design, and careful production.

Intelligence organizations are in competition with each other. They must study the market and develop its unexploited interstices. They must maintain small forces of decorous and highly intelligent salesmen who not only push the product and appraise consumer reaction to it but also discover new consumer problems with an eye to the development of new products. They must plan for the future.

Their organization must reflect these characteristics of business, and although both newspapermen and professors are said to be equally allergic to organization charts, the organizations must be set up by chart and operated with a decent respect for the chart. But at the same time they must strive for fluidity of structure; they must strive for the ability to shift power from an under-utilized unit to an overburdened one as unforeseen peak loads develop. They must not permit any unit to get a vested interest in some operation of forgotten importance. They must be willing to undertake heartbreaking reorganization when the balance sheet so indicates. They must be willing and able to undertake irksome and seemingly profitless tasks for the good will of their best customers, and above all they must not oversell themselves.

What I have said of intelligence organization is as true for peacetime as for wartime. Just because poor intelligence developing out of poor organization in a war has its highly dramatic penalties, there is no logic in assuming that similar penalties do not pertain to peace. Errors in the grand strategy of peace may not produce the spectacle of a needlessly disastrous battlefield, they sometimes produce something worse.

CHAPTER 6

CENTRAL INTELLIGENCE

As can be seen from the foregoing, the intelligence of grand strategy and national security is not produced spontaneously as a result of the normal processes of government; it is produced through complicated machinery and intense purposeful effort. In this and the following two chapters I will discuss certain aspects of the intelligence machine. I lead off with that of our own Central Intelligence.

On 22 January 1946 President Truman addressed a memorandum to the Secretaries of State, War, and Navy in which he directed "that all federal foreign intelligence activities be planned, developed and coordinated so as to assure the most effective accomplishment of the intelligence mission related to the national security." The memorandum continued, "I hereby designate you, together with another person to be named by me as my personal representative,[1] as the National Intelligence Authority to accomplish this purpose."

The memorandum went on: "2. Within the limits of available appropriations, you shall each from time to time assign persons and facilities from your respective Departments, which persons shall collectively form a Central Intelligence Group and shall, under the direction of a Director of Central Intelligence assist the National Intelligence Authority. The Director of Central Intelligence shall be designated by me, shall be responsible to the National Intelligence Authority, and shall sit as a non-voting member thereof."

With these words the President created for the first time in our history a formal and official central organization for

[1] Fleet Admiral Leahy was later named to this office.

strategic intelligence.[2] It will be noted that the Central Intelligence Group was not the usual sort of federal commission or board. It came into being in response to an executive act of the President as opposed to an act of Congress; and it depended upon three established departments of the government for personnel and funds.

Whereas this arrangement was commendable in that it permitted the speedy establishment of a central intelligence organization, it did possess obvious disadvantages. Prime among them was the disadvantage of uncertainty. Who could foretell when the "limits of available appropriations" of the contributing departments might be narrowed down to the point where the departments would be unable to "assign persons and facilities" in adequate supply? Who could tell when a Congress—otherwise favorably disposed to the central intelligence idea—might not destroy it by too great reduction of the budgets of the sustaining departments? In these circumstances what first-rate civilians would seek employment, what first-rate officers seek assignment there?

Lieutenant General Hoyt S. Vandenberg (now General), the second director of central intelligence focused his attention on the problem. Largely through his efforts, which extended throughout his directorship, central intelligence became legitimatized in an act of Congress. Title I, Section 102 of the *National Security Act of 1947* [3] establishes a Central Intelligence Agency and makes the matter of its

[2] During World War II the Joint Intelligence Committee of the Joint Chiefs of Staff carried out the strategic intelligence mission of wartime. Its several subcommittees and working committees did include representatives not merely from the Army, Navy, and Air Force, but from several of the civilian agencies as well—notably the State Department, the Office of Strategic Services, and the Foreign Economic Administration. To this extent the JIC was a kind of central intelligence organization but its sphere of activities was limited by the nature of its wartime mission. Its parent group, the JCS itself, never had an Executive Order proclaiming its formal existence.

[3] Eightieth Congress, First Session, Public Law 253.

79

budget one of the annual concerns of Congress. Let us examine the statute.

Perhaps first to be said is that it purported to close out, for the time being at least, a long argument as to the essential form that central intelligence should take. In the last days of the war this argument was at peak and centered around the basic question as to whether central intelligence should be a very large operating organization or whether it should be a kind of holding and management organization. The most extreme advocates of the operating-organization idea asserted that an agency which had an almost exclusive responsibility for the intelligence of grand strategy and national security would be the only kind to do a proper job. Whereas they did not propose to put departmental intelligence completely out of business, they did urge a central organization, which would conduct on its own, the functions described in current doctrine as collection, evaluation, and dissemination (or as I have defined them—surveillance, research, and dissemination). As such it could not help but envelop (or duplicate) a substantial part of the departmental intelligence functions. It would have a staff of appropriate size: very large. It would not be a part of a policy-making or operating department or agency of the government. It would be a vast and living encyclopedia of reference set apart from all such departments and agencies, and devoted to their service. Some of its proponents would have had it report to the Joint Chiefs of Staff, some to the President.

Around the advocacy of such an organization whirled the usual arguments for and against highly centralized administration. In my opinion these were peripheral to the real issues. In one highly significant matter the proponents of the large operating company had a strong case. It was: if thrust into the collecting phase of intelligence—especially the overt collecting phase—the new organization might do a better job than was currently being done.

The bulk of overt collection was then and is now carried out by overseas representatives of those departments of the government concerned with our foreign relations. The three service departments, as well as the Departments of Commerce, Agriculture, Treasury, Justice, and others send attachés; and the State Department, which stands in the forefront of all of them, sends its Foreign Service Officers and attachés. For reasons deeply rooted in tradition and administrative practice, the quality of this overseas surveillance and collecting force has been below standard. Some of its members have had too many other duties to allow for a good surveillance and reporting job; some have had the time and inclination but not the substantive competence; some have had the time and neither the inclination nor the competence. But let us not forget those who have been downright brilliant.

Now it is arguable that a new institution charged with this surveillance and reporting function would be in a strong position to break with departmental precedent and put a keen expert force in the field. The chance of better foreign reporting constitutes perhaps the strongest argument for highly centralized intelligence.

At the same time such centralization violates what to me is the single most important principle of successful intelligence, i.e. closeness of intelligence producers to intelligence users or consumers. Even within a single department it is hard enough to develop the kinds of confidence between producers and consumers that alone make possible the completeness, timeliness, and applicability of the product. There are great barriers to this confidence even when intelligence is in the same uniform or building or line of work. But how much more difficult to establish that confidence across the no man's land that presently lies between departments. It would be too easy for such an agency to become sealed off from real intimacy with the State, Army, Navy, and Air Force departments; to live in

81

relative innocence of their particular fears and of the small but significant changes in their objectives, policies, and plans. It would not be impossible for such an organization to misdirect its efforts, watch the wrong developments, and report on matters of small concern. Moreover, its remoteness from day-to-day departmental business would have a seriously adverse effect upon the applicability of its research product. And it may not be too much to say that directives to the departments from the President himself could not alter this situation. The departments which inevitably carry the chief responsibilities for the grand strategy would continue their own intelligence work and would remain aloof; they might not be entirely wholehearted in passing on to the agency the take of their own intelligence operations. They might be a lot less than wholehearted in passing on information which they were entitled to consider "operational information." [4] In matters of interdepartmental concern, such as those handled by the old State-War-Navy Coordinating Committee, each department could be counted upon to rely upon the knowledge produced by its own people. There would be

[4] Administrative practice likes to try to make a distinction between what it calls informational (or intelligence) communications and operational communications. In many cases the distinction is valid. For instance, a cable concerned with the payroll, leave, and travel of the Embassy staff, say, in Lima has operational but no intelligence importance. However, other cables which are primarily devoted to operations may have an important underlay of intelligence. Suppose, for instance, a communication comes in which asks for supplementary funds for travel. Such a request would normally require explanation and in the explanation might well be contained information of an important nature. Common carriers in Peru may have suddenly become inadequate or unsafe or unreliable—a fact which puts the mission at a great disadvantage. It must have special arrangements for its staff. If the recently developed trouble in public transport had not already been the subject of an informational report, the "operational" communication in question might be the only word sent home on the subject. And if this particular communication were held closely on the grounds that its content was primarily of operational concern, the receiving organization could be said to be withholding intelligence from the field.

little disposition to revere the opinions and facts produced by the agency just because it was *central*.

The National Security Act, as it applies to the Central Intelligence Agency, endeavors to meet this danger in a number of ways. One of them is to reject the idea of the large self-contained operating organization and to establish an agency primarily dedicated to the coordination of departmental intelligence. Let us examine the text of the act.

Its fourth paragraph (paragraph d) describes the function of the new Central Intelligence Agency. It reads:

"For purposes of coordinating the intelligence activities of the several Government departments and agencies in the interest of national security it shall be the duty of the Agency, under the direction of the National Security Council — [5]

"1. to advise the National Security Council in matters concerning such intelligence activities of the Government departments and agencies as relate to national security;

"2. to make recommendations to the National Security Council for the coordination of such intelligence activities of the departments and agencies of the Government as relate to the national security;

"3. to correlate and evaluate intelligence relating to the national security, and provide for the appropriate dissemination of such intelligence within the Government using where appropriate existing agencies and facilities:

[5] See Section 101 of the National Security Act. The Chairman of the Council shall be the President, or his designate from among its members. These shall be the President, the Secretary of State, the Secretary of Defense (see Section 202 of the Act) the Secretary of the Army (See Section 205), the Secretary of the Navy, The Secretary of the Air Force (see Section 207), the Chairman of the National Security Resources Board (see Section 103). With advice and consent of the Senate the President may from time to time designate other Cabinet members, the Chairman of the Munitions Board (see Section 213), and the Chairman of the Research and Development Board (see Section 214). Thus the new National Security Council replaces the former National Intelligence Authority as the interdepartmental organization to which the CIA is responsible.

Provided, that the Agency shall have no police, subpoena, law-enforcement powers, or internal security functions; *Provided further,* that the departments and other agencies of the Government shall continue to collect, evaluate, correlate, and disseminate departmental intelligence: *And provided further,* that the Director of Central Intelligence shall be responsible for protecting the intelligence sources and methods from unauthorized disclosures;

"4. to perform, for the benefit of existing intelligence agencies, such additional services of common concern as the National Security Council determines can be more efficiently accomplished centrally;

"5. to perform such other functions and duties related to intelligence affecting the national security the National Security Council may from time to time direct."

Let me pause briefly at this point. Certain matters are quite clear in this paragraph. To begin with the clearest ones first: The Agency will not have any police functions. The American public, which has rightfully feared any tie-up between intelligence and the police power and which upon occasions has been misled by irresponsible newspapers, can bury the specter of an emergent American Gestapo or MVD. Equally clear is the fact that CIA does not supersede departmental intelligence; CIA's task is to add to its effectiveness by coordinating it and supplementing it. That CIA cannot usurp functions more properly performed in the departments seems to be adequately guaranteed by its subservience to the National Security Council upon which sit the secretaries of the departments in question. Lastly it is very clear that CIA will have certain operating functions (subheadings 4 and 5) and that these are to be construed as either directly in aid of departmental intelligence or as an indistinguishable part of its general mission of coordination.

A little less clear is the matter of advising the NSC on departmental intelligence and of making recommendations for its coordination. Obviously CIA can advise and recommend only when it knows practically everything there is to know about departmental intelligence. This implies that CIA should have an unrestricted right of inspection, but no such right is vouchsafed by the Act. To be sure the next paragraph, (e), does consider inspection, but the inspection in question seems to be an inspection of intelligence (knowledge, the product of the intelligence activity) and not the departmental activity which produced it. It might be argued—and I imagine it has been argued—that the right to inspect the product conveys the ability to judge the operation which puts it out. But there is a considerable difference between this right of judgment and a right to inspection *qua* inspection. I should guess that anyone responsible for the awesome task of coordinating the intelligence of national security would sleep better if his inspectorial rights were stated a bit more carefully and fully.

Basic to all discussion so far is the meaning of the words "national security." As I have argued earlier, all of the aims of foreign policy or the grand strategy become inextricably intertwined. Is United States policy with respect to the UN a policy which emerges from our desire to promote a better world order or one which emerges from our insistence upon national security? Does our atomic energy policy emerge from the one or the other? Is our policy on the International Trade Organization undertaken in behalf of our material prosperity, a better world order, or our national security? I personally would not be bold enough to hazard a categorical answer to any of these questions, nor do I feel craven in not doing so. I find it hard to imagine the CIA being any bolder and I assume therefore that the intelligence functions of the Agency will in actual fact be considerably broader than a narrow construction of the Act's "national security" would have it. In fact I can only surmise that under the rubric of "national security intelligence" CIA will find itself in all reaches of the intelligence of high policy and the grand strategy. This, the Act does not spell out. Maybe it is not necessary.

The next paragraph (e) is dedicated to making sure that CIA has the ability to "correlate and evaluate intelligence relating to the national security. . . ." [6] It reads: "To the extent recommended by the National Security Council and approved by the President, such intelligence of the departments and agencies of the Government, except as hereinafter provided, relating to the national security shall be open to the inspection of the Director of Central Intelligence, and such intelligence as relates to the national security and is possessed by such departments and other agencies of the Government, except as hereinafter provided, shall be made available to the Director of Central Intelligence for correlation, evaluation, and dissemination: Provided, however, that upon written request of the Director of Central Intelligence, the Director of the Federal Bureau of Investigation shall make available to the Director of Central Intelligence such information for correlation, evaluation, and dissemination as may be essential to the national security."

The meaning of the paragraph is quite clear: if central intelligence is mandated to correlate, evaluate, and disseminate a certain kind of knowledge, and if it is not to produce this knowledge from scratch, then it must have access to the files of the organizations which do produce it from scratch. CIA must have the right to inspect (i.e. right to see the files) because it is unreasonable to require that CIA ask for knowledge by the title of the document it may appear in. Without the right of inspection CIA would be in a hopeless spot; it would have to ask the departments for knowledge the existence of which it did not certainly know. And in the event of a negative reply from the department it could never be certain that the department was

[6] See Article 3 of paragraph (d).

unaware of possessing the information, had not mislaid it, or was willfully withholding it.

In addition to the right of inspection CIA must also have the right to use the information which the departments produce from scratch. Hence the phrase: such intelligence . . . "shall be made available to" CIA.

The special position which the FBI enjoys among the other departmental intelligence organizations is noteworthy. If I read the lines correctly, CIA has no right of inspection in the FBI. When it wants information which it feels may be possessed by the FBI, CIA must ask for it in writing. In the best of circumstances this procedure constitutes a barrier between the two organizations, and in circumstances other than the best it can become an impenetrable wall.

To be sure the FBI's main function is peripheral to CIA's, and the bulk of information which the FBI produces from scratch will not be of interest to CIA. For instance, CIA is not likely to be concerned with any of the FBI's domestic intelligence in aid of its law enforcement duties. On the other hand, there are areas in which the FBI works which can be of immense importance to CIA. From the wording of the Act, whether or not CIA is informed of the FBI's knowledge in these areas would seem to rest too heavily upon such intangibles as good inter-agency relations and personal friendships.

Preceding paragraphs of the Act place the CIA in an appropriate interdepartmental milieu, provide for the position of its director, and make special provision with respect to its personnel.

Paragraphs (a) and (b) establish CIA under the National Security Council and deal at some length with the problem of the director. According to the text he may be either a commissioned officer of the armed services or an individual from civilian life. His salary is to be $14,000 whatever his previous status. This means that if he is of one of the services, he will draw his service pay and enough additional to bring him up to the full $14,000 amount. Furthermore as an officer he is removed from the chain of command: "he shall be subject to no supervision, control, restriction, or prohibition (military or otherwise) other than would be operative with respect to him if he were a civilian. . . . He shall not possess or exercise any supervision, control, powers, or functions (other than such as he possesses . . . as Director) with respect to the armed services or any component thereof. . . ." Having completed his tour as Director of CIA, his service may not put him under any disability for having been absent from service duty.

In making these provisions with respect to the director, Congress tried to overcome certain objections to entrusting the job to an officer of the armed services. These objections may be stated as follows: (1) The incumbency of a service officer is likely to be short. Furthermore it may be terminated at the very moment when a change in the top control will be most harmful to the organization. The reasons for this situation lie in the services' own demand for their best officers and in any officer's reluctance to separate himself too long from his service lest he damage his professional military career thereby. In stipulating the high salary (higher than any save that of five-star rank) plus the guarantees of no-disability for absence from a straight service assignment, Congress was holding out an inducement for long continuous tenure and protection for the officer who made use of it. (2) An officer on loan to CIA from one of the services, and *not* separated from the chain of his command might not be free to act in complete impartiality toward the other services represented in CIA—might have duties within his own service which would prejudice his wholehearted devotion to CIA. By specifically lifting him out of the chain of command Congress has tried to meet these objections.

But still Congress has not dealt with all objections—the ones which remain I will consider in the latter half of this chapter.

Paragraph (c) of the act gives the director the power to "terminate the employment" . . . of anyone in the Agency, "whenever he shall deem such termination necessary or advisable in the interests of the United States." The Director's power in this respect overrides guarantees of tenure written into civil service legislation. At the same time the present act goes on to say that persons thus terminated are to be under no disability in seeking and accepting employment elsewhere in the government.

This paragraph is dictated by the personnel problem which confronts all federal departments and agencies—intelligence and otherwise—charged with the national security. That employees in such organizations, and within the government at large, must be loyal and discrete goes without saying. But in the so-called security agencies (notably State, Army, Navy, Air Force, Atomic Energy Commission, FBI, and CIA) this is not enough. Certain of their employees and all of those of CIA must be in a special bracket of dependability. It can be argued that if a man has irregular habits or abnormal quirks of character he may be subject to pressures akin to blackmail; that if a man has near relatives living under the control of a foreign state he may be subject to similar pressures. Persons of these categories are not of as good dependability—or, as the phrase goes, are not as good security risks—as others, and a security agency might be well advised not to employ them. Once they are employed, the agency should be allowed to terminate their employment without prejudicing their employment rights and expectations elsewhere in the government.[7] What is true for the security agencies

[7] It goes without saying that a person with a primary and demonstrable attachment to a foreign power, or to an ideology inconsistent with that of the U.S., has even less reason for employment in a security agency or, for

in general is true of their intelligence compartments, and even more so for CIA. For unless CIA is known or believed to be the safest place in the government it will not have the full confidence of the agencies to which it is supposed to be central. And if it does not have this confidence it has no function. Therefore paragraph (c) of the Act is of vital importance to the very existence of central intelligence.

The framers of the foregoing paragraphs of the National Security Act have recognized three matters basic to the achievement of an intelligence of national security. They have recognized the fundamental importance of departmental intelligence and have not impaired it in the interest of central intelligence. They have recognized that departmental intelligence must be worked over ("coordinated" is their word)—by some higher power to make sure that it adds up to the requirements of national security. And finally they have realized that certain essentially operating tasks in aid of the total intelligence effort might better be undertaken centrally. That the framers did not spell out at length how departmental intelligence should be coordinated and how supplemented is certainly to be understood and applauded. The question is however, does the Act give CIA and its Director sufficient latitude to do a good job of coordinating and supplementing. To answer this question it is necessary to say what the good job in question involves. In the rest of this chapter I shall try to answer the question with respect to my notions of what the job calls for—first with respect to the *coordination or management* function.

The job of coordinating departmental intelligence activities is an important one. It is far more important than

---

that matter, anywhere in the government. But for the very reason that the problem of loyalty is so much broader than that of security in an intelligence organization a full discussion of it would not seem appropriate in a book of this kind.

the coordinating of the knowledge which these activities produce. For unless the coordinating agency can exercise some influence over what should and should not be produced, it is hard to see how coordinating that which is nominally produced will always be a remunerative operation. I feel therefore that CIA's primary task lies in some sort of oversight over departmental activities. Let me be clear about the departments and agencies in question.

In the first instance the departments in question are the four which have a primary responsibility for the national security, viz., State, Army, Navy, and Air Force. In peacetime, the Department of State claims, and generally enjoys, primacy in the field of foreign policy—which as I have indicated earlier, includes the maintenance of the national security as one of its objectives. Thus, at the present writing, intelligence activities of the Department of State are or should be of a high degree of importance under the CIA canopy.

In the second instance the departments and agencies at issue are those like Treasury, Commerce, Agriculture, Justice, the Tariff Commission, and so on, whose primary responsibilities lie in the domestic sphere, but whose share in foreign affairs is by no means negligible. As domestic and foreign policy becomes harder and harder to separate, even a department with the name Department of the Interior finds itself in foreign matters. Actually, Interior's Bureau of Mines does a good bit of observation and research on the mineral resources of foreign countries. The point is that after the big four there is a lesser group of twenty-plus organizations which contribute much to the totality of federal knowledge and which, therefore, fall under CIA's coordinative power. The coordinating task I have in mind requires that CIA follow six lines of administrative activity.

One, it must establish clear jurisdictions for the various departmental intelligence organizations. That is, it must define what subjects each will pursue and what subjects each will not pursue. For example, it might tell the Department of Agriculture to do a better job in foreign agricultural intelligence and tell the State Department to get out of that field. It might tell the Division of Intelligence in the Army Department to get out of certain aspects of economic intelligence and tell the Department of Commerce to take on this responsibility.

Two, having set up departmental jurisdictions, it would police them. The policing would have to be a continuous process and would have to be carried out with the greatest tolerance and wisdom. It would consist of three subactivities. *First*, it would deal with the inevitable expansion of one jurisdiction over into another. In this guise CIA would pursue needless duplications of function. I should like to stress the word "needless," and assert that all apparent duplications are by no means duplication in fact. People who shout duplication at the first sign of similarity in two functions and who try to freeze one of them out on the ground of extravagance often cost the government dearly in the long run. *Second*, CIA would see that every department was exploiting the entire area of its jurisdiction. By this I mean that a department would not be permitted to pick and choose the subjects within its jurisdiction and skimp on those it found distasteful or relatively useless for purely departmental purposes. No department could welch on its allotted responsibility and thus permit a gap to develop in the total picture. *Third*, it would have to enlarge certain of the established jurisdictions by the addition of new subject matter as it appeared and became significant to the national security. For example, responsibility for knowledge of space ships may one day have to be assigned to some department's jurisdiction.

Three, to return to my main lines of coordinative activity, CIA should run a continuing survey of departmental intelligence to see that its produce is up to standards of quality, and that the contribution which each departmental outfit makes to an interdepartmental project has the interdepartmental orientation. This is perhaps as important as the quality of the work itself, for without what I have called the interdepartmental orientation individual contributions will not add up. Nor can they be made to add up. The project manager in central intelligence will find himself forced to do a substantial part of the original work all over again and from scratch. As I will point out later this must be avoided at all costs.

Four, if a departmental intelligence organization should be in default, central intelligence must be ready to diagnose and help correct the trouble. For instance, on the theory that the intelligence requirements of top policy will be something larger than the sum of the requirements of departmental policy, and on the theory that the sum of normal departmental contributions to a given top-policy project falls short of the requirements, some department may well be judged in default of its obligation. It might be that this top project demands such a thing as a table of world tugboat tonnages and that the Navy Department had never before felt obligated to keep a tally of tugs. The Office of Naval Intelligence could not deliver. If such information were mandatory for the project, central intelligence should be ready to see that ONI got the funds and personnel to go into tugboat intelligence.

Five, central intelligence must manage directly or indirectly all interdepartmental projects. By such projects I mean studies which will require both surveillance and research along a very broad front and which will be destined for White House, Cabinet, National Security Council, and the Joint Chiefs of Staff. Projects of this sort will command the resources and skills of all federal intelligence and should be carried out under CIA responsibility. I have in mind such large orders as the Vatican in world affairs, the probable world growth curve of international

Communism, and the effect upon world power alignments of the new movements in the so-called dependent areas. It may be that central intelligence will have one of its own staff act as project supervisor, or it may be that the project supervisor is temporarily borrowed from a departmental intelligence outfit. In either case, the supervisor should be responsible in the first instance to the Director of CIA or his delegate.

Six, CIA should take cognizance of the personnel policies of departmental intelligence. It should be fully aware of the difficulties which civil service and the departments themselves occasion intelligence work. It should take an active part in seeing that the proper people are recruited and trained for departmental intelligence.

In performing these six types of coordinating activity, CIA should be guided by one high overriding principle—it should *stay out of primary substantive work*. CIA will have to staff up on a few men of highest professional competence in appropriate fields of study. It will have to have some outstanding economists and political scientists, some international relations specialists, some specialists in the military art. It will have to have a somewhat larger number of junior men who have begun to make their professional way. But as little as possible should this staff get into the creative substantive work. It should confine its activities to management of interdepartmental projects, criticisms of the departmental contributions to such projects, investigation of why such departmental contributions are inadequate or in default. Its job is what might be called policing the professional competence of the departmental outfits and continuously pushing departmental frailties back into departmental laps.

As soon as CIA departs from this principle, as soon as it gets into substantive work and itself makes descriptive or evaluative studies, it is in trouble. For when it does this, it becomes little more than a fifth major research and surveillance outfit. It enters into direct competition with its subsidiaries and at great disadvantage. It competes with them for professional personnel in a market which is already tight to the strangulation point. It competes with them in building up a library of basic documentation (see page 133 and following), and its lateness in entering this field puts it under enormous handicap. It has few consumers which are not also served by departmental intelligence outfits or by *ad hoc* combinations of them and thus it competes for consumers and consumer guidance. This guidance will be grudgingly given to an organization which is administratively separated from the consumer and which has no operating responsibility.

Competition of this sort will annoy and anger. Departmental intelligence will swear out the vendetta and through a few sordid and well-known bureaucratic dodges may negate CIA's whole program. Not that bad blood will not be created in the six lines of management I have proposed. I see plenty of it. But I do not see it enduring forever. For the role I have assigned CIA is a non-competitive role and one which the departments should come to honor once they have recovered from the original shock.

Some may argue that CIA cannot police substantive competence in the departments unless it has a staff which can beat departmental intelligence at its own game. By this they imply that CIA cannot keep up departmental standards until it is so strong a research organization that it is virtually the match of the combined strength of all the departmental outfits. With this point of view I cannot agree at all. I do not believe that a critic, to be constructive, must know everything that the person he criticizes knows. I do believe that a wise and experienced critic can poke holes in an argument or put his finger on soft spots in another's work without being the *technical* equal or master of that other. The kind of critic I have in mind is the elder statesman of his profession, the man who has

95

been through the mill of detailed duty or original work and who, therefore, has a high ability to discern the good and bad in another's work. He is a man who keeps up with his profession, in fact leads it, not by doing the chores of early and mid career, but by doing the ripe and reflective work of full career. I should expect that they—a dozen or so aided by perhaps a score of sharp assistants—would be civilians. Not only will civilians suitable for the job be more abundant, but as well, *the right ones* can move with high fluidity from service to service. Perhaps higher fluidity than an officer of one of the services. If more than a dozen of such were needed there is no reason to withhold them, so long as they clearly understood that their duty was criticism and direction, not surveillance and research.

The problem of recruiting a dozen such men is perhaps the key problem of the whole program I have laid down. Without them the program will not move. I believe, however, that they can be recruited but only under the following conditions:

1. The program which they are to inaugurate must have been fully thought through. More, CIA must have taken soundings in the National Security Council and made sure of its support. No men of the caliber I have in mind will take on a job of this sort until they have some clear notions on the chances of success.

2. If they are to be civilians then the leadership of CIA must be civilian. The National Security Act has obviated some of the disadvantages of military leadership, but it has not obviated the main one. This is that so long as an officer of the armed services is director of CIA it is almost inescapable that his immediate staff also will be of the military. It is likewise almost inescapable that he will set up his organization according to the familiar military staff pattern and will pad out the top echelon—it has happened often—with Army, Navy, Air Force, and Marine officers. Appointment to the top staff in this way is likely to de-

pend upon criteria such as appropriate rank, availability, and branch of service. Some of the officers will be there because they are colonels or captains not otherwise assigned and others will be there merely to maintain a service-by-service balance in the table of organization. Some of this group will have little professional competence in the specialized task of high-level intelligence and others may have little interest to boot. In short, the people to whom the civilian experts report and with whom they must work will be chosen on criteria far different from those to which the civilians themselves owed their own appointments. They will not regard this situation as enhancing the job, and no matter how good and great a man the Director, they will be recruited with difficulty.

Of course there is an alternative, namely, to have a military Director and to man the top coordinating echelon from the ablest men of the services themselves. I am not of those who assert the services do not possess officers of adequate professional training for the job. I know they do. I also know, however, that the services will be slow to assign such officers to intelligence and that the officers themselves will not be gay about the assignment. A long duty in intelligence is not the best way to advance in the military career.[8] Realize that the privileges and immunities with which Congress has invested the Director (should he be an officer) do not apply to other military men assigned to CIA. But suppose the services assign and the officers gladly accept the assignment and go to work. I submit that such a coordinating staff will have more trouble dealing with the military departments than a civilian group—and almost certainly more difficulty with the civilian departments. For instance, if someone is to investigate shortcomings of the Army's intelligence activities, he should be an army officer, not a navy or air officer. But it may happen that the right man for the job wears the blue

[8] In the next chapter, I deal with this problem at some length.

97

uniform. And if someone is to give unpleasant advice to State or Commerce, he had best not be a man in any color uniform. To create an all-military coordinating staff is to rob it of fluidity of action with respect to the services and prejudice its success with the civilian departments.

Let us suppose that CIA is civilianized as to leadership and does recruit its key professional coordinating personnel, what of the remaining problems? They are blockbusters. Take the question of defining the jurisdiction of a given departmental intelligence organization—say, the Army Department's Division of Intelligence.

Everyone would agree that Army Department positive intelligence should produce knowledge on the ground forces of foreign states. This is just about as far as the agreement will go. Ask the next question—"what is meant by ground forces? the force in being or the mobilizable force?"—and see what happens. The Army Department would hold that knowledge of the ground forces in being was only a fragment of what it had to know; it would argue that the force in being is only an inaccurate and misleading symbol of the total ground force which might be mobilized for war. It is against the potential force that our army must be prepared, not against the fragment in being. Now this mobilizable force is no simple thing, and to calculate its size and striking power no mere matter of military intelligence narrowly construed. As I tried to demonstrate in Chapter 4, calculations on mobilizable force are preponderantly based on knowledge of political, economic, social, and moral phenomena. To estimate mobilizable force or war potential, Army Department intelligence must spread far and wide over other departmental jurisdictions.

Suppose now that CIA moves to restrict the Army Department's jurisdiction and to make other departments—in this case State and Commerce especially—furnish it the political and economic knowledge to complete its calculation. Two howls will go up. One will go up from the Army

Department to indicate that it is not satisfied with the stuff it is receiving. It will say that what State and Commerce are handing on is inadequate or that it cannot be fitted into its kind of estimate. The other howl will go up from State and Commerce to indicate that their intelligence organizations are over-burdened with their own departmental duties and that they do not want the Army Department account.

Or, State and Commerce's howl will indicate that they would be glad to work for the Army Department if the latter were more specific in its demands. As matters stand, they claim, the Army Department is being overly cautious about the large project to which they are supposed to contribute. So long as they do not know the end-use to which their product will be put, they cannot turn out a satisfactory job. Indeed they may go further and say that this is the last time they will aid the Army Department if it does not take them into its confidence and give them the sort of guidance they require.

Such arguments back and forth will inevitably draw CIA deeper and deeper into the supervision of departmental intelligence operations. If CIA has the right men in its own employ this will be a good thing for the country. But it will not be so conceived by the parties of the second part. They will take it with poor grace, and CIA must be strong and competent to weather a five-year storm.

The trouble CIA makes for itself on these jurisdictional problems will be aggravated when it cracks down, say, on the State Department for an unsatisfactory contribution to one of its (CIA's) own interdepartmental projects. Its subsequent investigation into State's intelligence organization will, for a while at least, provoke bad feeling. State, as other departments, will have its difficulties accommodating itself to what it will consider an impairment of its sovereignty.

But CIA may improve its position with its subsidiaries

when it fights the good fight for them. If the State Department's poor performance were occasioned by a lack of staff, and the lack of staff by unreasonable budget-cutting, CIA's championship of more funds will win friends. This and the fact that department intelligence craves good top management may take some of the sting out of CIA's unpleasant activities. If it can bring departmental intelligence together as a team on broad intelligence problems which everyone regards as nationally important; if it can furnish first-rate interdepartmental project supervisors and good staff work, it can step on departmental toes and survive a good deal of departmental wrath. The fact that it is not competing with the departments will be one of the strongest points in its favor.

In the very best of circumstances the task I have outlined for the CIA of my choice would be an extremely difficult one. But the wording of the Act does not describe to me the best of circumstances. To begin with, it does not civilianize the agency by specifying that the Director must come from civil life. In permitting an officer of the armed services to hold the post the Act gives CIA a military aura. This may turn out to be a positive disadvantage, for in making possible an accumulation of military men at the top level, it will discourage the recruitment of professionally competent civilians at what I have called the coordinating level. Let us not forget that the subject matter of CIA's particular brand of intelligence is much closer to so-called civilian specialties than to military.

But as I have indicated, failure to have high-caliber civilians in the coordinating staff is not necessarily a disaster. The services have able people for the job if they (the services) are willing to assign them and keep them there for long periods of time. Let us assume that they do just this. Under these conditions has CIA everything it could ask in the way of statutory powers to do the job I have described?

I do not think it has. For the drafters of the Act have been too much preoccupied in the wrong direction. They have given CIA access to the product of departmental intelligence activities, but not to those activities themselves. In truth they have given CIA the right to make recommendations about the activities, but they have not vouchsafed CIA the right directly to investigate them. Under the Act, if CIA is to make such recommendations it will have to base them not on a direct first-hand knowledge of what these activities are, but upon a knowledge of them inferred from a study of their end product. This process seems unnecessarily devious to me—like leaving an auto's ignition switch off and propelling it by its battery and starter.

Suppose the director of CIA senses something wrong in departmental intelligence and suppose that, because of the limitations of the Act, he cannot make weighty and pointed recommendations to the NSC. Suppose the NSC is not impressed by the recommendations he does make. The director of CIA is none the less under the terrifying responsibilities of the Act. If he cannot get what he must have from departmental intelligence and if he has not the power to make departmental intelligence produce it, his way is all too clear. He must start producing his own intelligence from scratch. He must embark upon his own full-scale surveillance and research activities. And, as I have remarked, in so doing he will move into competition with the departments. Things being as they are he cannot expect to triumph; departmental intelligence, no matter how inadequate it becomes, has certain important and persistent advantages. The best he can hope for is a stalemate.

So far I have confined myself only to the first of the two chief functions of CIA, e.g. coordination. What of the second, the operating function? The nature of this is set forth in sections 4 and 5 of paragraph (d) of the Act. It consists of performing for the benefit of departmental intelligence those tasks which can best be performed centrally plus any other tasks that the NSC assigns it. The intent is clear and its chance of realization high. In its operations CIA will be working in behalf of the departments. Should CIA desire to go off on its own it must first obtain clearance from the NSC upon which sit the secretaries of the departments in question. They may be expected to show an appropriate amount of parochial interest in the departmental operations. That they should is just right.

In consonance with what I have said about CIA and the coordinating function, I repeat here: CIA's operating functions should not be in competition with the departments. Whatever the substantive product of these operations may be, it should be a product designed to fit a departmental intelligence requirement. Or, it should be a product to fit the requirement of some interdepartmental project. It should not be something which CIA fancies too important for departmental use, or too far removed from all departmental jurisdictions. For as soon as CIA operates and produces new substantive knowledge only for its own account, and as soon as it passes this knowledge on to some final consumer without making the departments party to the procedure, CIA is in substantive work. All of the woes which will beset it if its coordinating activities lead it to original and creative research, will beset it in this second case.

It seems to me that the worst thing CIA could do would be to set up operations in aid of a home research staff and to try to turn out supra-departmental knowledge without the partnership of the departments. Should departmental intelligence reach such a low estate that it was unworthy of CIA's confidence, then CIA's job would be to build up departmental intelligence—not try to supersede it. For if the Central Intelligence Agency insists on trying to perform the entire intelligence job and in so trying endeavors to reduce departmental organizations to impotence it will not succeed. It will emerge from the battle perhaps still an agency but not central, and it may not even warrant the name intelligence.

CHAPTER 7

DEPARTMENTAL INTELLIGENCE

B Y DEPARTMENTAL intelligence I mean the organizations within certain federal departments and agencies which are devoted to the production of intelligence (knowledge) of what goes oń abroad. There are a great many such organizations—perhaps twenty or more—but those of primary importance are, as I have already noted, within the Department of State, Army, Navy, and Air Force. It is these organizations—the State Department's Office of Intelligence Research and Office of Collection and Dissemination, the Army Department's Division of Intelligence, the Navy Department's Division of Naval Intelligence, and the Air Force's Division of Intelligence—which should in the nature of things produce, or possess the capacity to produce, most of the basic knowledge for our high-level foreign policy and grand strategy. The remainder is the product of the Central Intelligence Agency and of the other departments peripheral to the problems of foreign relations.

The job of any one of the big four is easy to describe theoretically—though as I indicated in the last chapter, very difficult to describe in practical terms. In theory the job should consist of describing, observing and reporting upon, and speculating as to the future of those phenomena in foreign lands which lie within the jurisdictional competence of the department. Thus our Air Force's intelligence arm should devote itself to foreign military aviation and our State Department's intelligence to foreign political and perhaps economic activities. The job which any one of the big four does will tend to be a double one. Ideally it will first produce all the knowledge required for enlightened departmental policy, and second, enough more of the same kind of knowledge to satisfy the requirements of national policy. This is to say that departmental intelligence has obligations both to the department which houses and supports it and to the councils of top national policy which lie above. This latter obligation may force an intelligence organization to produce knowledge within the department's sphere of interest of a breadth and a degree of remoteness that would not be necessary for straight departmental consumption. This is the kind of extra knowledge which the Central Intelligence Agency must have in order to carry out its program of long-range interdepartmental studies.

To perform the dual task departmental intelligence must have an organization and people to fill it. Let me speak of the people first. They should come first because the *proper* people constitute the single essential element. There is no substitute for them.

The people in any departmental intelligence organization are of several main categories:

First, and in common with all organizations there must be the administrative housekeepers—the people who see that the mail comes in and goes out, that the staff has working quarters and supplies, that the staff gets paid; that the multifarious regulations regarding leave, travel, efficiency ratings, and the working day are observed; that the classification of positions is in line with regulations of the Civil Service Commission, and that the budget gets prepared and presented in order and in time.[1]

---

[1] I will not discuss this group of people further because the problems surrounding them are problems by no means peculiar to an intelligence outfit. However, I am reluctant to leave the area of the administrative force in government work without some comments which apply to my own experience in intelligence, and I suspect, to many a civil servant in other reaches of the government.

On principle I would always find myself on the side of the advocates of administrative decentralization. I fully realize the penalties which a loose administrative organization imposes, but my conviction is that they are far less than the penalties of the other extreme—*a fortiori* in government, where the main administrative problems go back to the antiquities and obscurities of the Civil Service Statute. The lesser unit, or to use the

Next there is the clerical group. This is composed of the people who do the paper work for the administrators, but more importantly it also encompasses the people who put out and physically distribute the operation's end-product: the studies and reports and memos. I might go further and include all the various categories of reproducers: the mimeographers, the photographers, the printers of maps, the assemblers and binders of manuscript, and although it will not flatter them to be included here—the people who aim to present the language of letter and number in the language of picture.[2]

Next is the library group about which I will have more to say in the next chapter. As in any institution where research is going forward and where new knowledge is the end-product, they constitute the keepers of the physical accumulation of knowledge. They take in, as a result of their own and other peoples' efforts, the data of yesterday; they index and file it; they safeguard it; they dispense it

---

jargon, the lower echelon unit, of any government office which has no administrative agent to represent its case (and represent it with fervor and low animal cunning in the higher administrative office) is out of luck. The Civil Service system under its present jungle of rules and regulations must inevitably appear as not much more than a conspiracy against competence. The only way a low echelon unit can stay in business is to maintain its own paid administrative champion to fight its way through to the surface. Without a large amount of such decentralization and resultant combat there is the calm which settles over buried cities: the front office is beaten into line by the Commission and the survival of the unfit throughout the organization becomes the order of the day.

[2] With respect to these latter—the visual presentation experts—I find myself of several minds. There is no question that good diagrams and charts improve the understandability of certain kinds of text. There is also no question—to me at least—that certain other kinds of text cannot be illustrated, let alone improved in understandability, by such diagrams. The presenters themselves are not always of this latter view. Like members of any new and aggressive calling they often seem to be unaware of the limitations of their medium and highly reluctant to play the role of a passive service organization. If left to follow their own inclinations, they have been known not merely to essay the impossible in picture language, but also to start urging the professionals whose work they should be illustrating to change the wording and even the meaning so as to make it more amenable to their means of expression.

to the people who are putting the data together in new patterns and deriving from it new approximations to truth.

Next is the professional staff which, with my last group, is the crucial part of the organization. Without the professional experts there is no intelligence. These are the people who are students of the manifold aspects of life abroad I have described earlier. They are the social and natural scientists and the military experts who have a finger-tip feel for the ways of research and analysis, who are masters (or dedicated novitiates) of the tools and techniques of their particular bracket of learning, and to whom the discovery of new facts or new relationships between facts is a career. They are the people with wide screens of professional sensitivity whose organs of reception register and convey minute changes in the areas they have under surveillance—changes which would not register at all on a less specialized screen. They are the people who, stimulated by a minute change, automatically go into action to prove its importance or unimportance and its validity or invalidity. Further—who go into action equipped with the basic knowledge for research in their particular field. They are also the people who undertake research at the suggestion of a policy officer or a planner, the people who find out about the food situation in China for Mr. Clayton, or the broad outlines of the program which the Russian listener to the *Voice of America* wants to hear. They are the ones who furnish the knowledge for testing the feasibility of objectives and the knowledge from which policy and plans may be formulated. In short, they are the human element behind everything that is written in this book, and if they do not in actual departmental practice measure up to the specifications of this paragraph or do not perform the functions I have designated for them, *they should.*

My last group is the group of substantive managers who are in spirit and training at least a fraction of the professional staff set off for other duties. The job which they have to do is that of seeing that the output of the professional staff is specifically directed to the current problems of the department and to those of top policy; that the component pieces of the output, i.e. the studies or maps or reports or memos, will be produced according to the priority of demand for them; that the finished projects will be complete, balanced, and delivered on time; and that they will be delivered in a physical form most appropriate for the user. (You do not send a 200-page study to the White House when the request asked for a memorandum, nor do you send a memo to the operating officer who has requested an encyclopedia.)

To carry out this job the substantive managers must be exceptional indeed. For they must combine a high degree of professional ability with a high degree of practical sophistication and managerial talent. They must have professional standing in order to command the respect of a professional staff. That they have this respect and the good will which usually goes with it is of utmost importance. They will have great difficulty in obtaining either respect or good will without themselves possessing a reputation and a proven ability in an apposite field of systematic study. This experience in turn will favor their performance in another and almost equally important way: it will permit them a personal insight into the capabilities of the staff and a foreglimpse of the time necessary for the completion of a given project.

The other quality which they must possess is no less vital. It is the quality or qualities which permit them to move easily and informally among the policy people and planners of their own and other departments and to identify the intelligence requirements of the main problems which are at issue; it is the quality which gives them good judgment on the priority rating of the main problems, and which permits them to see precisely where the weight and power of their organization can be most effectively utilized. What I am describing is not what every professional gets with his graduate training; in fact he is likely not to acquire it anywhere. Generally he has to be born with it. It is good sense, discretion, tact, ability to get on with people, ability to lead and direct them, a knowledge of what makes the world go around, and an acute understanding of where the world is right now.

There can be no question of the importance of competent professional specialists and of this managerial control staff. Yet departmental intelligence often behaves otherwise. It often behaves as if the secret of success lay in ingenious organization, as if a subtle and complicated product could be turned out by inexpert people using foolproof jigs and tools. I hold that this is an egregiously mistaken notion; I hold that you cannot produce knowledge of a high order of subtlety and utility in the same way you produce Fords. If you follow the assembly-line principle and multiply the individual steps and stages of an intelligence enterprise to the point where each of them is so reduced in complexity that a non-professional employee can perform it, you will not get knowledge at the end of the line. You will get virtually nothing of value. You will continue to get next to nothing until the people who work at the rudimentary tasks also know a great deal about the whole process and are also able to work effectively at many of the advanced stations on the line.

The simplest example of what I am talking about is the habitual division of labor between a foreign language translation service and the analysis of the translated texts. There may be such a thing as foolproof translation, but I have seldom seen it. Language, being the blunt tool that it is, is capable of concealing the message it aims to convey to everyone except the man who is attuned in advance to its meaning. Just as some very wise men cannot read a timetable in their own language, so other equally wise men who have spent a lifetime learning and teaching a foreign language will find many things written in this language which they cannot translate. They can translate only those passages where both the foreign and American meanings are experientially familiar to them. The man who can render every shade of meaning of a foreign novel into our language will not necessarily be the man who can translate a technical article. Furthermore all the dictionaries in the world are not going to see him through his difficulties if he should try. He cannot translate the article until he has mastered its tricky vocabulary, which in turn means that he has, in some measure, mastered the subject matter. The point is that the intelligence officer who must rely on some-one else's translation of the materials he himself must analyze is at the mercy of the translator, and in my experi-ence few people who are satisfied with the dreary job of routine translation are ones I would choose to lean upon.

But the division of labor in the translation service is only one ready example among many. Separation of the collecting from the evaluating phase, and the evaluating phase from what is termed "research" on the organization diagrams are other parts of the same picture and even more open to question on the same basis.

The masters and doctors of public administration who draw the organization diagrams have seemed too often oblivious of this, as have high officials in departments which must perform a crucial intelligence mission. Service thought along these lines I find peculiarly hard to under-stand. It takes off from the premise that the line officer shall not become a specialist in any one kind of endeavor, and that the top brackets of the career, whether in staff or line, will be filled by officers with command experience. Although the services do tacitly acknowledge the impor-tance of specialization in such obvious matters as medicine or communications or logistics they do not give these spe-cialists parity with the line officer by guaranteeing them identical career opportunities. Paradoxically, where no institution is more aware of the value of staff work than the services and few institutions put such emphasis upon it, the officer with too much staff experience in his life or the officer who would choose nothing but staff work is under a disability cognate with that of the technical or professional specialist. The result of this line of thinking upon the intelligence function is to be regretted.

The general officer or flag officer in charge of intelligence at the general staff level of Army, Navy, and Air Force is almost invariably a man with distinguished command experience. By the same token, he is almost never a man whose whole life has been devoted to strategic intelligence. The people in his organization upon whom he places most reliance and who exercise greatest authority —his deputies, his operating branch chiefs, his staff advisers, and even sometimes some of his "experts," are almost certain to come from the same stratum of command experience. Those with a future in the service cannot afford to do too long a stretch in any specialized task—intelligence included—and the best of them, who in a few years of study and practice in a given intelligence area would become experts in every sense of the word, are the very ones who must move on. Behind them they may leave, in more or less permanent residence, the men who have become reconciled to not rising to the top. This is not to imply that these are necessarily always the least wise, imaginative, and active men in the service, but it is certainly to argue that they are not always the people of greatest wisdom and imagination, and the most active.

Given this situation—a situation in which personnel of the very highest degree of technical competence are needed but not forthcoming—it is perhaps reasonable that service thinking tries to produce a remedy in the organization diagram. On the principle that a crew of x men can bring a 16-inch gun turret to bear upon an invisible target and hit it by the deft but uncomprehending use of delicate and complicated gadgets, this thinking argues a similiar case for a similar division of labor in a problem, say, economic analysis. Break down the task into its simplest components and use as many men as you have components. With gunnery the solution works better than with economics.

The services have an extremely difficult problem on their hands. There is no escaping the fact that their prime obligation is to win the battles and the wars. One hundred and fifty years ago the state of the art of war was such that generally informed and intelligent men were adequately equipped to use the then relatively simple machines of war. At that time an overwhelming percentage of an armed establishment could take its place in the line and a very small percentage had to be withheld for setting up, maintaining, and improving the machines. In these circumstances the services could afford to frown on specialization, and they did so. But not a decade has passed in which the state of the art of war has not changed, and changed in tune with the growth of science and technology. Today an army, navy, or air force must still be able to put a winning force in the field, and at the same time employ the incredibly complicated new implements. So complicated are these that a service might dissipate its entire capability in learning their refinements and the nuances of their most effective use. There is a not unnatural apprehension in service opinion that unless one is on his guard, the armed forces will be under the control of the new gadgets instead of the other way around. Thus there is another of those well-known cultural lags which in this case is damaging to the services' professional specialists. The services realize they must have them, but they have not yet reached the point of putting a proper value on their talents. And until these special talents get the same opportunity for accomplishment, advancement, and acclaim which holds for line duty, the specialist's function will suffer.

Now strategic intelligence is one of the phenomena of war and peace which has advanced in complexity along with all the other machines and techniques. It is no longer something that a competent officer can do between two command assignments. It is a specialty of the very highest order and until the services recognize it as such and properly recruit, train, and reward personnel who make a career of it, they are certain to do an inadequate job.

But the services are not the only departments which are culpable. The State Department, for example, had no intelligence service by that name until the fall of 1945. (It had had some research units in recent years that did not survive for long.) The intelligence mission, in so far as it was carried out at all, was carried out by non-specialists who also had a thousand other things to do. Among the conservative element of the department, which was also the regnant element, there was little or no comprehension of what intelligence was and no disposition to support an intelligence staff. In fact when the Research and Analysis Branch of the Office of Strategic Services was transferred to the department by Executive Order (20 September 1945, to take effect 1 October 1945) it was vigorously opposed by the old guard. They did not want an intelligence outfit as such, although they did assert an interest in some of the personnel and the library. They urged the break-up of the inherited organization and the apportioning of its regional experts to the appropriate operating desks of the so-called geographic offices. Although this meant grave damage to the organization, Mr. Byrnes was prevailed upon to take the step.

Throughout the debate which preceded Mr. Byrnes's action, high officers of the State Department based their argument on one basic issue. According to their lights, they already had an intelligence organization in that they themselves were all intelligence officers. They therefore did not need—nor indeed did they want—an organization which might reach conclusions different from their own. To the extent that sensate beings usually know and think before they act, these State Department officers—some of whom were very able individuals—were correct in asserting that they were intelligence officers, but to the extent that they knew everything which they should and could have known before they acted, they were not. Of two important aspects of intelligence, they had time to do no more than an indifferent job of surveillance and no time at all for research. If an army had followed a similar line of argument and based its action upon it, it might have tried the Normandy landing with knights in armor or the reduction of the Japanese homeland by Greek fire.

Since Mr. Byrnes's decision, the situation in the State Department has changed considerably. One of General Marshall's first acts upon becoming Secretary of State was to reverse Mr. Byrnes and restore the department's intelligence organization to its original shape. If left thus and given the wherewithal to rebuild its staff, it would certainly have become of increasing value. But no sooner had the retransformation taken place than the organization began to be starved out. Its budgets have been clipped in the department and manhandled in Congress. The reductions have been sufficiently severe to have occasioned almost mortal hurt.

There are other civilian agencies which have a secondary role in foreign policy and which have more or less continuously given intelligence its due. Although they have not always called it by that name, and although they have not been able to maintain it at high level in every budget year, they have nevertheless demonstrated a thorough understanding of the problems. They have realized the importance of the task; they have had a decent respect for full and accurate knowledge; they have employed the right kind of professional people to produce it; and these people have been given an enlightened leadership. It is in some of the reaches of departments like Labor, Commerce, and Agriculture that one finds the encouraging element in departmental intelligence.

Let us assume that departmental intelligence overcomes the handicaps it is working under; let us assume that it recruits the right people and properly directs their efforts; that each departmental intelligence unit digs in in the area of that department's jurisdiction. The question is, can we expect that the sum of departmental intelligence will add up to the requirements of the grand strategy and the national security? It seems to me that we can expect this only if the coordinating and managerial job done by a central intelligence agency is of the same degree of expertness as that of the control personnel of departmental intelligence. In other words, CIA (in its coordinating function) is to the whole intelligence picture what the substantive managers (call them the Control Staff) of any departmental intelligence unit is to the departmental professional staff. It must do the same sort of job, though on a larger scale; it must have the same type of people, though better.

CHAPTER 8

DEPARTMENTAL INTELLIGENCE
ORGANIZATION:
TEN LESSONS FROM EXPERIENCE

IT IS virtually impossible to separate the substantive elements of a big subject like intelligence from the methods of setting up and operating an intelligence organization. In preceding pages although I have not dealt with administrative problems except as they arise in other contexts, I have touched upon many of them. In this chapter I will try to concentrate all that will be said of administration in its own context. The selection of the problems and my interpretation of them derives from my five years in war and post-war intelligence experience. As will be seen, I will not attempt to draw the master organization chart, nor will I attempt to cover all fields of administration. I will confine myself in the first instance to organizational problems which are characteristic of the intelligence business, and in the second to only ten of those. The general reader will perhaps forgive this sortie into shop talk; but if he prefers he may turn immediately to Chapter 9 and resume his way.

Problem No. 1: Should the basic pattern of intelligence organization be regional or functional?

The job of strategic intelligence deals with foreign countries and with the complex of the life of foreign people. Any people, and especially those of greatest concern to our strategic intelligence, have many patterns of behavior. They behave as military beings organized into armed establishments, as political beings engaged in putting their formal relations with each other into orderly form; they behave as economic beings providing their creature wants, and as social, moral, and intellectual beings giving play to their gregariousness, their consciences, and their minds. Strategic intelligence, which puts peoples under surveillance and investigation, deals with them in both national and behavioral guises. It deals with them as Frenchmen, Swedes, Russians, and Belgians, and it deals with them also as military, political, or economic beings. Furthermore it deals with combinations of them, acting, say, in their military or economic guises; Swedes and Russians as economic men in a trade agreement; Britons and Frenchmen as political men looking out for their joint security. The practical question is, how do you plot your organization so as to deal best with both the national and the functional phases of foreign existence?

The trouble begins with the customs of American education. Certain groups of people who become critical experts in a line of study specialize in a geographical area, or a region, or a single national state. Modern historians, geographers, and some political scientists, for example, tend to be regional in their specialization and aim to learn all about, say, Greece, or the Iberian peninsula, or Latin America. They learn the necessary languages of the primary literature, they learn the whereabouts and whatabouts of that literature, they travel in the area whenever they can, and they write books about it. In these books they often move from disciplines of which they are real masters over into others of which they are not. The analytical modern historian, for example, inevitably finds himself working in the area of the political philosopher, the economist, and the sociologist.

Other groups of people devote their time to functional study. Many economists and sociologists, for instance, are striving for the discovery of economic or social laws which will obtain for the Chinese as well as the Egyptian or Dutchman. They specialize in the subject "economics" or "sociology," and oftentimes they do it without nailing

117

their investigations down to any country or race of men. At these times they work in pure theoretical terms with no earthy frame of reference whatever. At other times, when they must have an earthy frame of reference, they pick the most convenient one: the U.S.A. These non-regionalists learn only the languages that their theoretical literature is written in; they may learn French or German in order to get at the untranslated economic and sociological treatises which they must keep up with. They seldom bother to learn any other.

In these terms, suppose that a prospective loan to Iran must hinge upon the chances of success of Iranian economic recovery. Suppose a strategic intelligence outfit is given the task of making an estimate of these chances. What sort of organization will best handle the job: an organization which has an Iran section in command of the project or an organization which has an economic section in command? The argument is virtually endless. The regionalists say that unless you understand the nature of the Iranian, his traditional behavior, the national myths he defers to, and the character of Iranian politics and society, no amount of theoretical economic analysis will provide the answer. The functionalists, or economists in this case, say that economic considerations override all of these things; that the Iranian economic problem is not substantially different from any other economic problem; that their (the economists') business is the analysis of this universal economic behavior, and that if the regionalists will loan them some staff to act as translators and legmen they will get on with the job.

Out of this dilemma one thing is plain: you must have people who know a very great deal about Iran in general (and, I would insist, can read the Iranian language) and people who know the field of economics. Which of the two groups should have command of the project is by no means so plain, nor is there a clear answer to the larger question as to whether the whole organization should be laid down along regional or functional lines.

Unsophisticated administrative thought tends to compromise along unsophisticated lines. Faced with the basic organizational problem, it divides the world into a series of regional units, known as the European Division, Latin American Division, etc., and divides the functional subject matter into another set of units known as the Economic Division, the Psychology Division, etc. The outcome of such compromise is immediate and total administrative chaos. It is an invitation, and one readily accepted, for major civil war. In those matters which have, say, an economic or psychological aspect and which also pertain to a group of people (that is, in all matters except those of unique concern to the functional theorist) regionalists and functionalists will line up in defense of their special competence, will bicker and snipe, and will often end by producing two separate analyses which may contradict each other.

To be sure, there are more subtle and elaborate compromises possible than the simple and frustrating one outlined above, but in my experience they were so complicated that they tempted human nature to disregard them and cut corners, and when they did work they worked because of one superhuman genius in a key spot.

The compromise which I find myself supporting is one which uses the regional breakdown as far as possible. That is: step one is to break the world up into four or five major geographical areas, step two is to break each of these into smaller geographical components. Thus you might have a Far Eastern Division, composed of four sections, one of which deals with Southeast Asia. Within the Southeast Asia Section you could have a Burma Unit and as many other units as there were countries in Southeast Asia. This would take care of the regional specialists. But the chances are good that you could not regionalize the functionalists

119

down to the level of a single country. Our system of education does not produce economists whose chief competence lies in the field of the Burmese economy. Hence there must be a compromise.

The economists, if possible, should constitute a group at the level of the Southeast Asia Section. If competent economists cannot be found for so stringent a regional specialty, they should be trained, and in the meantime grouped at the level of the Far East Division. But in my view, the more one defers to the shortcomings of American training and the larger the geographic area one uses for the grouping of the functional staff, the more administrative grief one is piling up. Ideally, for many of the most important phases of strategic intelligence, the regional and functional expert should be one and the same man. The ideal Burmese unit should be made up of people, each one of whom could handle every complex and technical problem of Burma's existence, whether that problem were political, social, economic, legal, military, or what have you.

The compromise which I have advocated will appear to the functionalists as virtually no compromise at all. They will regard it as a distinct victory for the regionalists. But I believe that an essentially regional pattern should prevail for three reasons. They are:

One. The business which an intelligence organization must perform is predominantly national or regional business. Foreign policy and grand strategy seem in the first instance to deal with other states and groups of other states.

Two. The bulk of the primary data coming in or already available in the file or library is from a national source and deals with national or regional problems. Statistics, official reports and publications, observations, critical reviews, the press, monitored radio programs, and so on in very large measure follow the pattern of the world's political boundaries and appear in the official language of the state in question. The units of value and quantity in

120

which things are measured are likewise apt to follow a local national usage.

Three. The insights which are jointly reached into the significance of trends in a region will often be more valuable than what might be called eclectic insights arrived at by merging the work of an economist who was thinking "economics" and a political specialist who was thinking "region." To illustrate: if an economist who is thinking the *French* coal problem works with a political man who is thinking *French* politics the result is likely to be a better result than otherwise.

For these reasons, intelligence organizations which have essayed the non-regional or functional arrangement have found it practically inoperable. One very important organization finding functionalism thrust upon it was impotent until it was able to jockey, say, all Latin American work to its sociological division (which thereupon did little but Latin American political, economic, social, and military intelligence), all Far Eastern work to its political division, etc. The functional names on its various units were merely cover for the regional organization beneath.

As our institutions of higher learning go in for their so-called area programs, the aims of which are to produce exactly the kind of expert I have placed in my ideal Burma unit, the administrative problems of intelligence organizations are bound to become easier. We may look to the day when staff will be satisfied with the place it occupies on the organization chart and when it stops its silly jabber about the superiority of its special discipline. In the meantime, awaiting the appearance of these paragons, the formula for the best temporary solution is to set up a straight regional organization, to mix regionalists and functionalists (and mix them at the lowest possible administrative level), to make them sit next and work next each other, and finally to offer every prayer and inducement to them to respect and absorb the other man's professional competence.

This solution disposes, on paper at least, of a very large part of the classic regional-functional row, but by no means all of it. What remains is:

Problem No. 2: How to handle matters which defy regionalization?

In any strategic intelligence operation (as in the conduct of foreign relations themselves) there are problems which are impossible to handle on a regional or national basis. I refer to such things as the developments in international law, the United Nations, and other straight international organizations. There is a second range of problems which is international in nature though not so purely international as the above. These problems still have their distinctly national nuclei. They revolve around such institutions as the World Federation of Trade Unions (which is an international organization superimposed upon many national components) the Catholic Church, and the Cominform. There is still a third group of problems which are international only in the sense that they are multi-national; such matters as world trade and finance, transportation, food, and a number of key strategic commodities, such as rubber and oil.

An intelligence organization must handle all three sorts of problems. It must be doing a surveillance job on what is happening in these fields and it must be prepared to put a research team to work on them. A straight regional organization will not be able to do either. There must therefore be some sort of functional co-organization which is ancillary to the main regional show.

There is a simple principle which should govern the establishment of this functional staff. The units which deal with problems which have least connection with national states (my first category) can be properly built to the size necessary to handle the job by themselves, calling on regional sections when needed. The units which deal with problems not so purely international as the former (my second category) should be kept at minimum strength relying more heavily upon appropriate regional personnel. The units which deal with problems which are essentially multi-national rather than international problems (my third category) should consist of no more than one or two high-grade specialists whose main job is to needle the regional units and coordinate the regional effort. Furthermore these third-category units should be restricted rigorously to the subjects in which the intelligence organization has an important and primary responsibility.

From the above, the principle which I urge in the establishment of the functional part of the organization is a principle of *beware*. Beware lest the functional units, which had to be formed, grow to the point where they are a menace to the smooth working of the regional staff.

If this principle is followed and the functional units are kept in a secondary but highly specialized position, the organization will find itself confronted with still another category of job for which it provides no formal organization. The handling of this last category is my next problem.

Problem No. 3: How to handle those problems of a multi-national nature for which the organization provides no full-time functional supervisor or coordinator?

The kind of problem under discussion here is a very common one in the intelligence business; it arises from such phenomena as the Franco-British defense pact, the rebellion in northern Greece, the emergence of the Viet Nam Republic, or the racial issue in South Africa. In each case the situation involves the competence of more than a single regional unit.[1] The Greek problem, for example, to be properly dealt with, should be studied by the Greek, the Yugoslav, the Albanian, the Bulgarian, the U.S.S.R., the British, and probably the Turkish experts. It will demand a good amount of political, economic, social, and military expertise on all these national fronts. It will surely demand the knowledge of the man or men who are functionally specializing in international communist movements. How is such a project undertaken?

The answer is that that it is undertaken on a purely *ad hoc* basis. Let us assume that an important consumer has asked for this study. Once formally accepted by the top managerial or control staff, which weighs it against other commitments and assigns it a priority, it is handed on to a project supervisor. He should be the man with the largest amount of substantive knowledge of the subject, who also is the best manager and coordinator and editor. Let us say he is chief of the Greek unit, or, if personnel problems are acute, a utility special assistant to the division chief for such assignments. He meets with people from other units, blocks out and breaks down the total task, farms out the pieces, outlines the length and formal structure, and sets the deadline. When the pieces are done and the final paper is being put together he bosses the work directly if he does not actually do it himself. He is the champion of the finished job; he sees to its clearance with the top managerial or control staff, its reproduction, and its dissemination to the important consumer and to other people who he knows will find it most useful.[2] Next week he may be

---

[1] I will deal with the large problem of dissemination at greater length later on.

[2] I am assuming that no single unit will have exclusive responsibility for both Britain and France, nor will any single unit have responsibility for the several states directly and indirectly involved in the Greek situation, or for metropolitan France and its far eastern colonies, or for Britain and all its dominions.

exclusively on his own region or country again, or he may be a minor member of another *ad hoc* team.

The task of the top control staff throughout this procedure is one of greatest importance. To begin with, they must pass on the relative importance of the project; they must see that the organization's totality of relevant competence is brought to bear upon the subject; they must stand behind the project supervisor in ironing out differences of opinion; they must critically examine the finished job for the way it is presented (length, language, completeness, etc.); and they must try to feel out and identify substantive soft spots even though they themselves may not be specialists in matters Greek.

Of their services the working staff is sometimes likely to be contemptuous and to hold that they do nothing but throw their ineptness in the way of the struggling professional. But the fact is that all professionals are not themselves any too realistic about the kind of work they are doing. They pay the well-known academic penalty for their expertness: they are often cavalier about deadlines, they are sometimes overly precious in matters of small practical concern, they are sometimes capable of blurring the crucial point or points at issue or burying them in irrelevancies. It is the job of the managerial staff or Control to introduce, where necessary, the corrective of utility and applicability to the problem at hand. This leads to:

Problem No. 4: How is effective control exercised without jeopardizing the accomplishment of the mission?

First let me say that Control is the crux of successful operation, and that successful control demands a kind of hard-boiledness which a staff of substantive experts often finds not merely distasteful but almost unsupportable. Control is thus quite justifiably placed in this list of prime administrative problems.

As has been noted elsewhere, Control must concern itself with the following chores:

1. From knowledge of what is going on in the world of policy, plans, and operations, it must see that the intelligence program is in line. This involves:

    a. Seeing that appropriate foreign activity is kept under special observation and that interesting leads are systematically followed up.

    b. Seeing that research is undertaken on problems which need illumination and that the totality of the outfit's relevant resources is brought to bear on these projects. This means that Control will know, in so far as such things may be known, the agenda of affairs of state and will undertake to have useful knowledge prepared in advance of formal action.

    c. Seeing that regular and special surveillance and research are programmed according to the priority of their importance.

    d. Doing some thoughtful anticipating of problems beyond the horizon.

2. Arbitrate disputes among the professional staff in mid-course.

3. Review and criticize the finished product from the point of view of its form and probe it for possible inaccuracies or want of balance.

4. Maintain standards of excellence for all work.

5. See that the finished product is reproduced in appropriate form.

6. See that it is properly distributed and that a record is kept of recipients.

Now in virtually every one of these tasks, Control may and sometimes does develop friction with the professional staff. For example, there is ample room for dispute as to who best knows the score and who thus is best equipped to set priorities. The professional staff which is continuously close to world developments may feel that its inside knowl-

126

edge of events furnishes a better basis of judgment than that which is afforded to Control.

Or consider the situation when Control vetoes the undertaking of a project on the ground that the subject is inconsequential. It may be that the unit which wishes to do the project is working on a quiet part of the world, where all projects are of a relative unimportance. If the professionals are capable and devoted men, this is one fact which will certainly escape their attention: their work to them must inevitably be the most important thing in life. All right, Control may reply, let them work on their low-priority jobs—they have nothing better to do—but they must also expect low priority on clearance, reproduction of their product, and its distribution.

Or again, let Control raise an eyebrow at what it considers impolitic language or let it doubt the soundness of a substantive conclusion and see what happens. The professionals are being questioned in the very field where they are, formally at least, entitled to regard themselves beyond criticism. They will always be indignant at what they call the tampering or tinkering of some lesser expert.

But the fact is that the professionals are a long way removed from the freedom of the institutions of learning from which they sprang, and which they reverence, and although what they have to offer to intelligence is its single priceless ingredient, they cannot expect to enjoy the same sort or degree of freedom under the driving practical obligations of government service. There is thus a tremendous inherent conflict between the very terms "professional staff" and "Control." How can it be ironed out?

I doubt if it can ever be completely ironed out so long as Control is established at the top of the administrative pyramid. The ideal solution seems to me to push the control function back down the hierarchy as far as possible. If this were done, each professional unit would have its own control officer. Almost certainly he would be a trusted member of the professional staff who had a flare for the control job. More than likely he would be the unit chief. If this were the case at the lowest administrative level, the unit chief would be devoting half his energies to parochial problems and half to the control problems of the whole large organization. The chief at the next level up would be spending less energy on his local problems and more on the general ones. The chiefs of the top echelon would constitute the governing board of all the control officers, and the director of the organization, the ex officio chairman. In such a fashion the people closest to the realities of substantive work would be setting the standards of excellence, the procedures, styling, etc. But there are enormous practical difficulties to such a solution. I list them:

1. Budget wizards would immediately perceive a lamentable duplication of work and would insist on centralizing the function and reducing the staff necessary to perform it.

2. If by a miracle the budget wizard did permit it, there would be the problem of the relationship between the small unit chief and his control officer (if the two jobs were not merged in the chief). After all, the control function is of highest importance and the unit chief could ill-afford to delegate it.

3. If he did not delegate it, he would have to perform it and his other duties as well. This would mean that he had more to do than one man should be asked to do. In fact there probably are not enough capable men for this sort of job to fill the vacancies.

4. If capable men could be found they would not be likely to accept the salary which Civil Service prescribes for a low-level unit chief.

In spite of these practical difficulties, the decentralization of the control function seems to me wholly worth striving for. Nothing that I can think of will better thrust responsibility upon those who should be carrying it.

But if we abandon the idea of decentralizing for the moment and cope with the situation in its practical realities; if we agree that Control must, even if temporarily, be centralized at the top, there are some principles which it would do well to follow.

First, as already noted, the personnel of Control should have as many of the professional gifts of the professional staff as may be. If Control is made up of people who have gone through some professional mill, have standing in their own right, have respect for the professional achievement of others—and if in addition, they have had intelligence experience at the working level—the curtailments which they impose upon staff freedom will be taken with much better grace. *Per contra,* with rare exceptions, nothing will make their necessary activities more unpalatable to staff than that their previous experience or field of specialization was remote from the pursuit of knowledge. If they are not entitled to an honorary membership in the club, dissidence and resignations (or applications for transfer) will follow in their tracks.

Second, Control must continually police the amount of paper work it requires of staff and see that it is kept at a minimum. If professional staff is not everlastingly compelled to fill out forms, write memos of defense, maintain over-elaborate bookkeeping of its efforts, participate in complicated paper procedures, etc., it will accept the more important regulation from Control with far less animus.

Third, Control must be able to demonstrate its utility by the swift performance of its job. It must act promptly in its authorization of projects, in its clearance of projects, and in its reproduction and distribution of the finished product. Furthermore, in the interests of speed it must be willing to break its own rules.

If Control can be properly manned and if it will spend part of its efforts in restraining its natural bureaucratic tendencies it may look to much more effective relations with staff—and pleasanter ones.

The preceding four problems had a string of continuity running through them; the next six are not so closely connected to each other.

Problem No. 5: What is the most effective administrative arrangement to govern the performance of a field force?

It goes without saying that the proper conduct of the intelligence business requires a force on foreign duty. Intelligence cannot make good on either its surveillance or its research function unless it can physically project part of itself out to the places where things are going on and where the raw materials of understanding are being produced. Without a field force of its own, any departmental intelligence organization will lose a needed sense of reality and immediacy. Ideally this force should be engaged in whatever type of activity is required to deliver the goods: overt, clandestine or both. And if the force in question were engaged in both kinds of activity, it should of course be under a single management. Were such an arrangement possible, the overt staff could furnish the clandestine with the specifications of the missing pieces. And on the other hand the clandestine staff could not only furnish the overt with such pieces, but more importantly, could pass on new hypotheses which it acquired in its subterranean wanderings. Perhaps to gain these advantages some countries have set up departmental field forces which engaged in both overt and clandestine activities. The Soviet Union's embassy in Ottawa sheltered the representatives of five home departments (a sixth was about to join) who among other things presumably engaged in both open and

130

secret intelligence work.[3] But perhaps, again, such countries set up such joint activities because they are innocent of the difficulties and blind to the risks.

The realities are wide of the ideals. As is demonstrated by the Soviet experience, the risks of disclosure of clandestine activities were large and when the break occurred the entire Ottawa mission was discredited. Not only this, but much more significantly, all states beyond the curtain now felt justified in putting Soviet missions on their soil under restrictions which they might not otherwise have chosen to impose. Needless to say the restrictions imposed adversely affect the permissible overt intelligence activities. Thus it would seem necessary to recognize the risks of such combined activities and to require that clandestine activities in the fields be cleanly separated from overt. This being the case, in the succeeding paragraphs I make the separation and will confine myself to the problems of the overt departmental field force.

The administrative problem with respect to such a field force arises from the following circumstances:

First, the actual man who is sent out, say to Great Frusina, should be a member of the professional home staff handling Frusinan matters.[4] To be effective in the field

[3] Report of the Royal Commission . . . June 27, 1946 (Ottawa, 1946) pp. 12-17 and esp. 19-29. The home departments represented were: The NKVD (Security Police), Central Committee of Communist Party, The Commissariat of Foreign Trade, the Red Army, and of course the Commissariat for Foreign Affairs. The Navy was probably about to place its own representative.

[4] On this point I will not yield an inch. The worst disfavor that can be done an intelligence operation is to send to the field personnel who are specially recruited for field duty and ship them out before they have worked their way into the bosom of the home staff. Field men should be home men who also have the outgoing, adventurous, and worldly qualities which a foreign assignment demands. They should know without thinking what the main problems of the home staff are, what it does not know, what it must find out, what it needs in the way of physical materials procurable only in Great Frusina, etc. They should know personally, and, if possible, they should like and admire the members of the staff they are leaving behind. Even under these conditions the problems of perfect understanding are not negligible.

he must maintain the closest possible relations with his home unit.

Second, the large organization (of which the Frusinan unit is a small part) which sends the man out to Great Frusina will be sending other men to other parts of the world. To handle the housekeeping of such an operation it will be forced to set up some sort of central administrative unit in the office of the chief of the organization. Furthermore, in as much as the man in Great Frusina may find out things about Pakistan which should be brought to the attention of the home Pakistan unit, and the man in London pick up data of interest to the Far East Division, there will be an administrative reason to interpose a substantive unit alongside the administrative one. This latter unit will see that all interested consumers of the end-product of field work are served. Thus the front office of the large organization comes to have a dual administrative stake in the field operation.

Third, when the field man arrives in Great Frusina he acquires a third boss. This is the chief of the U.S. official mission there, who in turn reports to the Secretary of State and the President.

The problem is how to maintain the close personal contact between the field man and the chief of his small Frusinan home unit—which is absolutely vital—and at the same time keep the other parties to the triarchy satisfied. To this problem I have no sure answer; in fact I do not think there is one. The hope is that human understanding and cumulative experience in making adjustments will bridge the inherent difficulties. This will be done more readily if everyone involved in the transaction realizes the ultimate importance of keeping the Frusinan professional staff as closely and informally tied to their field representative as possible, and makes every reasonable effort to accommodate and further that relationship.

Problem No. 6: Is there a library function in a strategic intelligence organization?

The answer is, yes.

An intelligence operation which has the attributes of both the large metropolitan daily newspaper and the large research foundation handles an enormous amount of incoming physical material. In its newspaper guise it receives a continuous flow of regular and irregular reports from its own field staff, some of which come in by cable and some by pouch. It is also likely to receive similar reports from other intelligence outfits in roughly the same line of work. It subscribes to the intelligence equivalent of the news services—the best example of which is the government-operated monitoring service which handles popular foreign radio programs. Pretty much as a matter of course it receives, on an exchange basis, the finished output of other departmental organizations which are following and studying conditions abroad. There are many other items in this general category covering the tonnage of classified and unclassified documentation that flows into Washington from all over the globe.

In its research-foundation guise, it deliberately and consistently procures other materials which its program of research makes essential. It subscribes to a wide range of professional journals, foreign newspapers, the official publications of foreign governments, officials and unofficial statistical series, and so on; it also keeps up its collection of standard works of reference, and the most important new books on subjects of peculiar interest. It has a call upon the Library of Congress and has inter-library loan arrangements with the great libraries of the country.

The problem is whether or not all these functions and some others should be handled in one central place, and whether or not that one central place should also be the repository for the physical materials. It is my conviction that one unit should handle these functions and should be the curator of what comes in. In short, I am an advocate of a central library of all the materials (maps excluded) which an intelligence organization needs.

A central library of the sort I advocate may consist of several separate parts: one part would be made up of unclassified printed books and magazines—this collection is a highly specialized one; it consists of the standard works of reference and the new technical publications not readily available elsewhere. A second part might be composed of photographs; a third and most important part consists of classified documentary materials of all sorts. The library, no matter how many parts it has, has the following tasks:

1. It acquires materials as a result of its own activities. This means that it procures such things as the latest foreign year books and gazettes and statistical annuals and directories; it procures the record of foreign parliamentary debates and other official publications of foreign governments which bear upon the mission of strategic intelligence; it procures foreign newspapers and technical journals. In this sort of procurement it has had the advice of the professional staff at home and in the field.

It also collects classified documents. It knows, for example, that practically all State Department cables (the non-administrative ones) are important; it knows that nearly all attaché reports and studies of foreign situations by other federal departments and agencies like the Department of Agriculture and the Tariff Commission are important. It knows that everything put out by this or that other intelligence operation is important. The library endeavors, therefore, *on its own* to procure all such materials. It will place blanket orders wherever it can and get the entire official output of a large number of organizations whose line of work is similar. In addition, when a member of the professional staff asks that such and such a document be obtained—naming it by source and subject, if not title—the library gets busy.

2. It registers such documentary materials and by circulating a daily mimeographed sheet informs professional staff as to what has come in.

3. By rigorous organization rules, by policing, cajolery, and every other device it endeavors to intercept similar materials which the staff has acquired on its own, and to register them as any other document. The professional staff will acquire such materials through its personal contacts with opposite numbers in other organizations. Often they are working papers, or notes, or memoranda not considered suitable for routine distribution. Often they are what might be classed as operational as opposed to informational papers and therefore inappropriate for outside scrutiny. There is a very large amount of this kind of material which the senior staff member will come by; it is likely to consist of his most valuable stuff.

The library should be allowed to register, index, and reissue it to the acquiring staff member on what amounts to permanent loan.[5]

4. It indexes all materials no matter how acquired on standard 3 x 5 library cards according to place of origin and subject. It gives each document a file number and a place in the central file. A meaningful indexing operation is the most valuable and costly part of the whole library business. Unless it is performed, there is no library in the real sense of the word. There exists nothing more than a formless accumulation of paper.

5. Upon call it delivers to professional staff such items as they require for their work, and keeps track of where these items are. If some other staff member later wants the document, the library recalls it or otherwise arranges for him to see it.

A library which operates along these lines will not be

[5] See p. 137, Problem No. 7.

arrogating to itself functions which properly do not belong to it (see the next problem, number 7), will be doing a clean and simple service job, and will in time build up a large volume of indexed materials. Such a collection is one of the most valuable assets of the organization.

Problem No. 7: Should there be a separate administrative unit for collection and dissemination?

Before hazarding an answer to this question it would be well to define the terms.

By collection is meant the *exclusive* right to procure for the use of professional staff all the raw materials which it needs. It means not merely the collection of the items which I have noted with respect to a library's collecting activities, but all other items. For example, a collecting unit, upon being informed that professional staff is going to do a study on the Iranian Tudeh Party's views on the Arab League, has the duty to collect information on this subject which will answer every conceivable question the mind of the Iranian specialist can pose. Thus collection in this sense involves collecting as any good librarian (of books) fulfills that function, and also collecting as a professional researcher collects after he has exhausted the static resources of his library.

By dissemination is meant the exclusive right to distribute to consumers: (a) raw materials which the surveillance people pick up in the field or at home,[6] and (b) the finished product as turned out by the professional staff.

In my view, to establish a collection and dissemination unit with those duties is little short of preposterous. With assignment of an exclusive collection function I find myself at greatest variance. For it is one thing for a library to do a good job of acquiring basic stuff of general utility (like State Department cables and embassy reports), and

---

[6] These may be the reported observations of attachés, photographs, maps, newspapers, books, magazines, etc.

quite another thing to vest in a librarian the exclusive right to acquire all the materials which, say, Mr. Jones, an Iranian specialist, will need to do his study of the Tudeh Party and the Arab League. It is quite another matter to require Mr. Jones to communicate to a collector what he thinks he will need to do his study. And it is quite another matter to make it administratively difficult, if not impossible, for Mr. Jones himself and in person to call on people in other government agencies and leaf through their files on Iran.

The collecting phase of research cannot be done once and for all at the initial stage of a project; the collection phase pervades all the other phases, and indeed is the phase which is never completed; and the only man to do the collecting of data (beyond obvious materials) which he cannot name by title is the one who knows what he is looking for. Should there exist a man in the library unit who was so great an Iranian expert that the professional Jones could make his wants known without giving a lecture course on Iranian life and politics, then this man should not be on the library staff. He should be on Mr. Jones's staff.

It will be argued that unless collection is centralized two calamities will result: one, professional staff will unsystematically canvass outside sources of information and as a result of uncoordinated and repetitious requests for the same material will antagonize these sources. Two, professional staff, upon acquiring materials through its own collecting efforts will tend to set up its own small library and hoard materials which other parts of the organization should have.

There are answers to both of these points.

One, anything that professional staff can ask for by specific designation should of course be procured by the regular acquisition methods of the library, provided the library can act with speed. Materials that professional staff cannot specifically designate, it must acquire itself. In these circumstances there is bound to be certain unavoidable duplication of requests. But this is not necessarily the unpardonable sin—especially when it results in a higher level of accomplishment. I have long felt that the man who makes a profession of blustering with indignation every time two people from the same agency make identical calls upon him would be more suitably employed elsewhere.

Two, professional staff will in fact tend to build up its own library. This is as it should be. On the other hand professional staff is the first to realize the advantages of having its private loot registered and indexed by the library. It may then get it back and in most cases keep it forever. Certainly not all private loot will be registered, and the organization will suffer accordingly, but that portion which is not turned into a central file will be relatively unimportant. Constant effort on the part of management and fast registration and return of such materials will keep the quantity small.

What about the dissemination function? First, what about the dissemination of the so-called raw material out of which the finished product is built up. Should it be disseminated in raw form? I see no reason whatever for the outside distribution of this material in its raw form. Let me be clear about the words "outside" and "raw form."

By outside I mean *outside* the parent intelligence organization. Of course it must be circulated *inside* the organization and circulated with speed and system. The prompt and effective routing of incoming data to the home surveillance and home research people is one of the library's prime jobs. But I do not feel that routing this material in the raw form outside is doing anyone a favor.

By raw form I mean as it comes in—precisely as it comes in. A certain amount of it which the professional staff regards as appropriate for outside distribution should be

sent out after it has passed the critical review of the reigning experts. The rest should be described on a daily or
weekly bulletin by source or subject or both, and outside
persons interested in it should encounter it first in this
bulletin. If they wish to see an item of interest let them
come around and draw it out of the library.[7]

Admittedly there are disadvantages which such a procedure imposes on outside users, but the disadvantages are
small compared to those attendant upon an indiscriminate
circulation of everything that comes in, in its original
form. In the present state of affairs when the field work
is done by far too many inexpert people and when their
virtues are likely to be calculated in terms of the bulk of
paper they send in, there seems to be good reason to establish some sort of high-grade professional screen through
which the raw material must pass on its way out. In Chapter 10, I touch on this problem again.

Second, what about the dissemination of the intelligence
organization's finished product?

That the daily or weekly summaries, the reports, studies,
maps, etc., are delivered to people with policy, planning,
and operating responsibilities should be and is a matter
of gravest concern to every person in the organization. It
is a function of ultimate importance. There are two reasons why it should not be placed in the hands of a special
collection-and-dissemination unit and why it should be
placed in what I have earlier called Control.

Administratively speaking, Control must know where its
goods are being sent and how received. It has, hands
down, the first claim on the records of distribution and

[7] This indeed is a system widely held among established intelligence
organizations. There is, however, within most of them a continuing pressure on the part of the library staff to send out the raw stuff before it has
been vetted by the professionals. This pressure is part of the same phenomenon which gets an aggressive library unit into the "Ask Mr. Foster"
business (see above, p. 28). People who are close to the handling of incoming stuff, its registration, its indexing and filing, have a pardonable
desire to show off a bit.

receipt. If the keeping of such records is placed elsewhere, Control must still have its duplicate set. Hence it would seem reasonable to vest the whole job in Control. Secondly, Control is closer to the professional staff than any other unit, and Control and Professional Staff together know more about the substantive side of the job than anyone else. Together they know more about the problems which the work is designed to serve, and hence more about the people who are dealing with the problems. Their continual striving for the *applicability* of their knowledge automatically put them in close touch with the potential users. Thus there is a sound substantive reason for them to perform the dissemination of the finished product.

In terms of the reasoning in the above paragraphs, I find it impossible to accept the concept of an administrative unit to handle exclusively the collection-and-dissemination functions. Collection of materials which can be designated by name or place or origin can be and should be collected by the library; other materials must be collected by professional staff. The dissemination of both the raw materials and the finished product is a matter in which the professional staff has such an intimate stake that it cannot be excluded. My own answer to the problem is a skillful and active library and a small distribution unit attached to the office of the chief of the organization where it will have close contact with Control and the professional staff.

Problem No. 8: How should the biographical intelligence function be performed?

Acquiring knowledge of personalities is one of the most important jobs of an intelligence organization. It is also an enormous job. The ideal biographical file would have tens of thousands of names [8] in it, and against each name

---

[8] A huge problem in itself is to decide which tens of thousands of the world's billion possible names are to be included. It is, however, not an administrative problem and I will not go into it here.

a very wide variety of data. There must be a wide range of data because there are so many pertinent questions always being asked about people. What sort of man is he? What are his political and economic views? What are all his names and when was he born? Can he speak English? Who are his intimates? What are his weaknesses? How long is he likely to hold his present standing? Where was he in 1937? Etc.

These questions and literally hundreds of others show that the perfect biographical note must include a large amount of cold factual information and a large amount of critical appraisal. The users of the note likewise partake of this two-way division of interest. A great many of them want to know nothing more than the exact title of the man's present job or his rank or his street address. Another group of users must know his probable chances of becoming the No. 1 man in his party, army, company, or church; his probable sentiments on the local sugar situation, on Mr. Bevin, or on the Christian faith. The first set of users does a considerable part of its business by telephone; the second by more or less formal request. In these terms the administrative problem begins to take shape:

One, a large amount of factual data must be assembled on a large number of people. Since much of this is a scissors-and-paste job it can be performed by people of clerical-plus status.

Two, these factual data must be in a central file where they can serve the use of the telephone customer. But since it is impossible to say where factual data begin and end and impossible to guarantee that all telephone customers will request only factual data, *all* biographical stuff should be kept in this same file.

Three, the critically evaluative part of the biographical note is beyond the competence of the clerical-plus group engaged in snipping biographical dictionaries and current newspapers.

141

The problem is, do you maintain the central file and build up the biographical staff with high-grade professionals; or do you break up the central file into its regional components and make the regional surveillance and research units keep up their parts; or do you try some compromise?

It appears to me that if the first course is adopted, i.e. build up a large and complete biographical staff or Personalities Unit, two evils result: one, since it is ridiculous to try to divorce people from the things that they do, the Personalities Unit is likely to become a cluster of small regional research units which duplicate a good part of the business of the main regional show. Two, it is very poor practice to try to stop this duplication by telling the regional units of the main show that they shall not have professional knowledge of the personalities of their respective areas.

If the second course is adopted and the whole operation decentralized to the main regional units, there are two other evils of equal magnitude: one, loss of the advantage of a central file and central telephone service. Two, the kind of professional management which is characteristic of the main regional units will not have adequate enthusiasm for the scissors-and-paste part of the job and will not give it proper emphasis.

Some sort of compromise is the only way out. The file must be kept together, the Personalities Unit must furnish the clerical and clerical-plus help; and the regional units must recruit high-grade professionals for their share of the burden. There is no good reason why these specially-recruited people should be the only ones in the regional units to work on biographies, nor that they themselves should work exclusively on biographies, but there is every reason to insist that whatever the circumstances they or their professional equivalents put in the requisite hours on biographical business. In the face of a tight deadline on a more compelling project there will always be a tendency temporarily to starve biographical work by merging the biographers with other staff. This must not happen.

Problem No. 9: What is the best disposition of the map problem?

The map is one of intelligence's most useful tools and most useful vehicles. It is of paramount importance to the work of the professional staff and it is the most dramatic and direct way of presenting a certain large block of their findings. Thus there are at least two aspects to the problem of maps which an intelligence organization must confront. The first of these is the problem of a map collection; the second, the problem of map-making or cartography.

Consider the collection first. It should consist of all the maps produced anywhere in the world which contain the latest data suspectible of presentation on a map. This is a large order. Few intelligence organizations come within shouting distance of the goal, but they strive for it with what resources they can muster. For the ideal map collection is one of the most powerful reference works imaginable. It tells the political specialist how the Communist vote in Brazil's last election was geographically distributed and what the new administrative divisions of the U.S.S.R. are; it tells the economist where the population of China is concentrated and why new industrial development in Turkey is improbable. It tells the strategist about terrain and the logistics man about supply channels.

The administrative problem is, who makes the map collection and who takes care of it? Is it the job of *the* library or is it the job of a special map library?

The answer seems clear in terms of the second map function, the cartographic or map-making function. An intelligence organization worthy of the name must make maps. It must make them as illustrations for its studies and various other sorts of presentation, and it must make them for their own sake. Generally speaking, the type of map which will be turned out is known as the small-scale specialty map; that is, it is not the kind of map suitable for planning a military operation, or a railroad right-of-way, or an artificial port, or an irrigation project. It is a depiction of data or of a situation which has a geographical significance and which at the same time can be accurately and strikingly presented on a stylized replica of a part of the globe's surface. To make such maps the cartographers must have someone else's maps for the reference data they may contain, and other information which they or the regional staff dig out of gazetteers, books, and documents. In other words, cartography is one of the largest users of the map collection: without it cartography could not operate.

The answer to the administrative problem thus begins to emerge: the map-collecting and the cartographic functions must be kept together. Should both be put under the library? I see no reason why they should; in fact I see many reasons why they should not. Chief of these is that certain phases of cartography are high professional skills which involve a great deal of the very kind of research which the rest of the professional staff performs. There is no good purpose served by putting a high-powered research operation under a service operation. Secondly, and perhaps just as important, it takes more than an ordinary talent to collect, index, and curate maps. A great deal of professional know-how is required, and the best of the map collectors are likely to be geographers and cartographers of considerable standing. If their task is regarded as a simple library-clerical function they will not want the job, and without them the map collection will be a sorry thing indeed. Thus the only conclusion I can reach is that all map duties should be kept together and given the same administrative autonomy as the largest regional unit. This

144

is not a perfect solution, for there is bound to be some overlap and perhaps a row or two between the regional units and cartography's research commitment, but this cannot be helped. Alternate solutions seem to carry a far greater cargo of difficulty.

Problem No. 10: How to maintain a professionally competent staff under the Civil Service Act and under conditions of budgetary stringency.

The intelligence agencies of the regular departments of government are operating under the jurisdiction of the Civil Service Commission and are subject to its regulations. Civil Service legislation aims to provide for the impartial selection of persons best qualified to fill government jobs, and none will challenge the validity of this purpose. Unfortunately, this ideal has not been attained.

During the war, manpower was scarce, needs were great, and expediency required that individual agencies be given a fairly free hand in selecting their employees. If you had a position to fill in an intelligence operation and found a man who seemed to fit your requirements, the chances were you could offer him the job. It was unlikely that he had, or was interested in, civil service status, but that did not matter.

In these circumstances, and with funds for an expanding organization, a good staff could be maintained. Keen, aggressive, and competent people were willing, even anxious to join up. Once in, they attracted their colleagues, and the weight and prestige of the intelligence organization snowballed. It came to be called a "good outfit" and annual requests for funds were apt to find added favor among the budget people and Congress.

Even in those days it was very difficult to fire and replace people who for one reason or another were unsatisfactory. The organization needed to expand, not only to take on added functions, but also to make room for new and better people to do the jobs neglected by the incompetents. After the war was over, economy in the federal budget became a political issue: few people were willing to admit that the intelligence business needed approximately as large a staff in peace as in wartime. In addition, the civil service regulations began again to be applied with full force.

Throughout the government, including its highly specialized intelligence outfits, standard reduction-in-force procedures were followed wherever reduced budgets made it necessary to reduce staff. In general, these procedures provide that employees with the slimmest rights of tenure shall be the first to go. It has happened many times that valuable employees have been dismissed and other people of a lesser order of competence stayed on. The least valuable people—those who are virtually unemployable outside of government—busily consolidate their grip on tenure and take advantage of all the rights which accrue to them under the system.

When vacancies occur they must be filled by persons who have the highest qualifications in terms of the civil service rules; these may be people who have just been released by other agencies, and often they fit poorly the jobs to which they are shunted. Only in high-echelon positions and in those requiring the greatest specialization is it possible to appoint men of outstanding professional qualification if they have never taken a civil service examination or never worked for the government.

Good people in intelligence are naturally discouraged by this situation. Many of them are insecure in their own jobs, no matter how good their performance has been, and all of the others are worried by actual or prospective loss of good staff. Their concern, when communicated to the outside, becomes the cause for outside bidding for their services. Business, industry, their former employers and colleagues in various forms of non-governmental service begin considering them as available and begin making at-

146

tractive offers. Two forces of disintegration are now working in concert on the most valuable people. They are
being nudged from within and beckoned from without.
Their loss is a catastrophe to federal intelligence work.
It is virtually impossible to find their replacements anywhere in the country. The only remedy is an heroic one—
highly specialized personnel, such as the professionals in
an intelligence organization, must be immune from ordinary civil service regulations. I fully realize the heresy of
such a suggestion, but unless some special provision is
made for intelligence, the whole question of the preserva-
tion of the democratic way may itself become one day
somewhat academic.

The above are by no means the only administrative
problems of the intelligence business, but they are problems on which much experience has been accumulated
in recent years—at great expense in grief and taxpayers'
dollars.

PART III
INTELLIGENCE IS ACTIVITY

CHAPTER 9

INTELLIGENCE IS ACTIVITY

IN THE language of the trade, the word intelligence is used not merely to designate the types of knowledge I have been discussing and the organization to produce this knowledge, it is used as a synonym for the *activity* which the organization performs. In this chapter and the next two I will discuss intelligence as activity, or perhaps better, as process. My primary concern will be the large number of methodological and other problems which are characteristic of the intelligence process. But before coming to these problems I should deal, if only briefly, with the process itself.

The knowledge, which I have been calling strategic intelligence, serves two uses: it serves a protective or defensive use in that it forewarns us of the designs which other powers may be hatching to the damage of our national interests; and it serves a positive or outgoing use in that it prepares the way for our own active foreign policy or grand strategy. But the important thing to grasp is that, no matter what the diversity of use to be served, the knowledge at issue is produced by the process of research.

Sometimes research is formal, highly technical, and weighty; sometimes it is informal, untechnical, and speedily arrived at. Sometimes a research project requires thousands of man-days of work, sometimes it is done in one man-minute or less.

The research process, especially that of strategic intelligence, is initiated in two chief ways. When the policy people or planners of our government begin formulating something new in our foreign policy they often come to intelligence and ask for background. (They should do more of this than they actually do.) In their request for this or that block of knowledge, they stimulate the intelligence force to embark upon a piece of research and a course of specially aimed surveillance. There is, however, a second way in which the intelligence force comes to initiate research. This is through its own systematic and continuing surveillance of what is going on abroad.

So important is this general surveillance that it is often conceived of as separable from research. I do not think it should be so conceived. Let me discuss it further.

Surveillance, as I am using the word here, is the observation of what goes on abroad and the deliberate attempt to make sense of it. The actual physical observing process takes place in foreign lands and at home; it can take place overtly or clandestinely or both.

In foreign countries we carry it on through a multitude of open-and-above-board officers—some civilian, some military—whose duty is to keep eyes and ears alert and report what they learn. These officers are the foreign service officers and attachés which I have mentioned earlier. Each of them has his field of special interest and competence, whether it be political, military, commercial, or cultural affairs, etc., and each is supposed to keep himself and his principals at home posted within this specialty.

Some foreign governments supplement the work of their overt officers of this type with espionage activities; that is, they send out secret agents, or undercover recruiters of secret agents, to discover and report on matters which would be difficult to discover overtly. If you would like a sample of how such activities are established and how they operate, read Richard Hirsch's *The Soviet Spies*,[1] or the *Report of the Royal* [Canadian] *Commission . . .*[2] upon which it is largely based.

Not all surveillance activities take place abroad; some

[1] New York, 1947.

[2] *Report of the Royal Commission . . . to Investigate the Facts relating to . . . the Communication . . . of Secret and Confidential Information to Agents of a Foreign Power, June 27, 1946,* (Ottawa, 1946).

very important ones take place at home in the intelligence headquarters. Queer as it may seem to observe a foreign country from a home observation post, there are several reasons for this apparent paradox.

First, there must be surveillance at home purely and simply as a matter of convenience. For example, what the official French radio beams on the rest of the world is a matter of considerable interest to us; we should like to know the content of its political news and commentary. It does not follow, however, that we must set up a complete radio-monitoring operation in every city of the world. The technical difficulties would be great, the large staff necessary to run such operations would be ill-received by some of the countries, and the costs would be tremendous. Hence, that extremely important surveillance organization known as the Foreign Broadcast Information Branch is established at home. Its monitoring stations pick up the most significant programs; the home office transcribes them, translates (and sometimes abstracts them), reproduces them, and sends them around to officers of the government. Departmental intelligence organizations are, of course, the chief beneficiaries.

A similar case will hold for official use of the large amount of foreign news which correspondents of our domestic press gather and cable home to their papers. Sharp newspapermen, though they have no connection with the intelligence work of our federal government, are important observers of foreign affairs and important, though inadvertent, contributors to the surveillance activity under discussion. Wise is the government not to try to intercept their dispatches at the point of origin, but to let them land in the home cable rooms of our domestic papers and put the content to official use. Doing the business this way means that an intelligence operation engaged in overt surveillance will have to have some small force at home which follows the best foreign news.

153

There is a second reason for home surveillance activity. It is based upon the proposition that anything being hatched abroad to our detriment has about it a conspiratorial air: it is being hatched in secret and there are several people or groups of people party to it. In the world of international relations these parties to the conspiracy may be residents of half a dozen countries, and the story of what they are up to, if ever pieced together, must be pieced together from fragments supplied from the half-dozen different national sources. For example, what Franco was considering at a given moment might be less available from Madrid sources than from those of Mexico City, Buenos Aires, Lisbon, Bayonne, and Rome. This is not to argue that Washington is the only place where surveillance should take place, but it is to argue that given the complicated nature of the modern world, there must be a listening and observation post and clearing house in a central spot.

However conducted—overtly or clandestinely, abroad or at home—surveillance serves two vital functions: It tells us when another state is contemplating a policy or an action hurtful to our national interest. In this role it stimulates the production of the defensive-protective knowledge necessary for our security. It also tells us what we must know about affairs abroad if we are to implement our own active outgoing policies. In this second function the surveillance force has collected, observed, and reported the wide range of phenomena which I described in Chapters 2 and 3 and without which strategic intelligence would have little content of current importance.

In talking of surveillance there is always the danger of portraying something entirely passive. Surveillance sounds like sitting back and awaiting the impression. But surveillance worthy of the name must be vigorous and aggressive. It must be aggressive in that the observer covers as much ground as possible, seeking to expose himself to a maximum number of phenomena; and more importantly, it must be aggressive in that the observer does a maximum amount of following up his impressions of these phenomena.

So long as I use the imprecise term "following up" I am on safe ground with the general reader and the intelligence brotherhood. It implies checking on the accuracy of sources, comparing divergent accounts, and gaining perspective by broadening the field of inquiry, finding new leads—out of all of which emerges a proposition which seems the truest of all possible propositions. Now I would like to call this process of following-up by the more precise term of "research" and say that a certain kind of research must accompany the surveillance activity. This research is a systematic endeavor to get firm meaning out of impressions. Surveillance without its accompanying research will produce spotty and superficial information.

Research has a greater importance than merely supplying the cutting edge to surveillance. It has a role entirely its own—in the service of the outgoing positive aspects of policy. In wartime it produces the knowledge of enemy strategic capabilities, enemy specific vulnerabilities; it produces the knowledge of the political and economic strengths and weaknesses of the enemy; it produces the knowledge of the physical plant which the enemy is using for war-making. On such knowledge our own offensive military plans were based. In peacetime, it produces the kind of knowledge of foreign lands that you would like to have if you had to decide whether to sponsor a European economic recovery program and then to defend it before Congress and your fellow countrymen.

Research is the only process which we of the liberal tradition are willing to admit is capable of giving us the truth, or a closer approximation to truth, than we now enjoy. A medieval philosopher would have been content to get his truth by extrapolating from Holy Writ, an African chieftain by consultation with his witch doctor, or a mystic like Adolf Hitler from communion with his intuitive self. But we insist, and have insisted for generations, that truth is to be approached, if not attained, through research guided by a systematic method. In the social sciences [3] which very largely constitute the subject matter of strategic intelligence, there is such a method. It is much like the method of physical sciences. It is not the same method but it is a method none the less.[4] It can be

[3] I am including the science of military strategy as a social science along with social psychology, economics, politics, sociology, geography, anthropology, history and others. It is worth noting that the intelligence of physical science and technology has a very heavy overlay of social science. For example, it is a very important matter to know precisely where Country Y is in its development of new fuels, vaccines, or weapons, and presumably only a man well-versed in the appropriate exact science is competent to handle the technical details of this intelligence problem. But just as important, possibly even more so, are the predictable effects of such developments upon the nation which produces them. If Country Y has found a new fuel which will revolutionize its aviation industry, has Country Y the desire and the cash to go through this revolution? And if Country Y does go through the revolution, what will be the results upon her commercial aviation policy, her attitude in foreign relations, etc.? These latter questions are of greatest importance and the answers to them do not necessarily lie within the province of the physical scientist or engineer. The answers are the stock in trade of the social scientists. Any foreign country working on the U.S. in the atomic age should be every bit as concerned about how our possession of the bomb and other atomic energy secrets will affect our own domestic and foreign policy as it should be in trying to find out our highly technical secrets. I should therefore expect the U.S. Division of Country Y's central intelligence outfit to employ a few scientists who are trying to find out how we do it and a larger number of social scientists to put their findings into the proper political, social, and economic contexts.

[4] It is often pointed out that the method of the social sciences differs most dramatically from that of the exact sciences in the enormous difficulties they encounter in running controlled and repetitive experiments and in achieving sure bases for prognosis. In spite of these great disadvantages, social scientists go on striving for improvements in their method which will afford the exactnesses of physics and chemistry. Some of the physical scientists, like President Conant of Harvard, while respectful of the "impartial and objective analyses" achieved by the social scientists would dissociate the two methods. They feel that the method of social science is so different from that of the physical sciences (for the reasons given above and others) that to try to make the two cognate is only to confuse. To quote Mr. Conant, "To say that all impartial and accurate analyses of facts are examples of the scientific method is to add confusion

described in any number of ways. For instance, one could easily paraphrase the discussion of the physical sciences (as set forth by President Conant of Harvard) and say that the method of the social sciences involves the development of new concepts from observations and that the new concepts in turn indicate and lead to new observations. But to expand this admirably simple formulation so that it would fit the special case of the social sciences would perhaps be less useful than to spell out another which is specifically designed to meet the present requirements.

In this other formulation seven steps or stages are recognized:

1. The appearance of a problem requiring the attention of a strategic intelligence staff.

2. Analysis of this problem to discover which facets of it are of actual importance to the U.S. and which of several lines of approach are most likely to be useful to its governmental consumers.

3. Collection of data bearing upon the problem as formulated in stage 2. This involves a survey of data already at hand and available in the libraries of documentary materials, and an endeavor to procure new data to fill in gaps.

4. Critical evaluation of the data thus assembled.

5. Study of the evaluated data with the intent of finding some sort of inherent meaning. The moment of the discovery of such meaning can be called the moment of hypothesis. In reality there is rarely such a thing as one moment of hypothesis though some students of method, largely as a convenience, speak as if there were. Nor can it be said categorically at what stage in the process hypotheses appear. One would be pleased to think that they

---

beyond measure to the problems of understanding [physical] science." (James B. Conant, *On Understanding Science*, New Haven, 1947, p. 10.) However Mr. Conant, as a chemist, is chiefly concerned to avoid confusion in the field of pure science. The social scientist has a very different concern.

appeared at this, the respectable stage 5, but in actual practice they begin appearing when the first datum is collected. They have been known to appear even before that, and they may continue to appear until the project is closed out —or even after that.

6. More collecting of data along the lines indicated by the more promising hypotheses, to confirm or deny them.

7. Establishment of one or more hypotheses as truer than others and statement of these hypotheses as the best present approximations of truth. This is the last stage and is often referred to as the *presentation* state.

At each of these stages two sorts of methodological problem arise. One sort is characteristic of all systematic research in the social sciences, the other derives from the peculiarities of intelligence's research activities. To put it another way: strategic intelligence has a set of methodological problems all its own which are relatively unknown to the social scientist at work in his university. My principal concern in the next chapter will be with this class of special methodological problems.

CHAPTER 10

SPECIAL PROBLEMS OF METHOD IN INTELLIGENCE WORK

STRATEGIC intelligence confronts difficulties at each stage in the method discussed in the last chapter. As I have said, these difficulties are not general to all research in the social sciences; they are peculiar to intelligence work. In the next pages I will discuss them stage by stage.

The word "problem" can cause some confusion. I use the word frequently and in two quite different senses. These I will tag throughout as "methodological problem," by which I mean a problem characteristic of the method of trying to establish a new approximation to truth, and "substantive problem," by which I mean a problem in the actual subject matter of strategic intelligence. As an example of a "substantive problem" consider the strategic stature of the Chinese Communists; as an example of a "methodological problem" consider the means you would employ to get the basic data on the Chinese communists' military establishment.

1. Stage One, the appearance of the substantive problem

The substantive problem in strategic intelligence can emerge in three principal ways.

a. The substantive problem may emerge as a result of the reflections of a man employed to do nothing but anticipate problems. In actual fact, the intelligence business employs all too few of such men. But suppose there are such men; their job is to ask themselves the hard, the searching, and the significant question and keep passing it on to professional staff. An intelligence operation should be bedeviled by such questions, and a substantial part of its work program should be concerned with getting answers. A Pearl Harbor disaster is to be ascribed in no small measure to the absence of some unpleasant and insistent person, who, knowing of the growing animus of Japan, kept asking when is the attack coming, where is it coming, and how is it coming? [1]

The methodological problem involved here is a very slight one, on the surface, at least. It consists of devising the means by which such anticipators will be sure of formulating good substantive problems. The only answer lies in picking a man who already knows a good deal about the substantive area in which he is supposed to ask questions, and who has an inquiring mind; and then see to it that he has ready access to every scrap of new incoming evidence on it, access to everyone who knows about it, and freedom from other burdensome duties. But if you go below the surface and ask, how does one come to ask oneself good questions, you start down one of the main roadways of epistemology. It is not my intention to do so.

b. The substantive problem can emerge when surveillance makes one aware of something unusual. For example, suppose the people watching Great Frusina learn that that country is expanding its Christian mission program in the Belgian Congo and that it has named a certain Brother Nepomuk as aide to the new director. If surveillance is sharp enough to recognize the unusualness of this shift in a minor part of Great Frusinan policy it has initiated a substantive problem which may be very important when followed up, or it may be of no importance at all.

The methodological problems here are very similar to those just touched upon: how can surveillance assure itself

---

[1] See Seth W. Richardson (General Counsel for the Joint Congressional Investigating Committee [on Pearl Harbor]), "Why Were We Caught Napping at Pearl Harbor?" *Saturday Evening Post* (vol. 219, no. 47, May 24, 1947). Mr. Richardson documents the proposition which is generally accepted.

of spotting the unusual, the really unusual? How can it be sure of putting the finger on the three things per week out of the thousands it observes and the millions that happen which are really of potential moment? The answer is the same as the former one: procure the services of wise men—and wise in the subject—and pray that their mysterious inner selves are of the kind which produce hypotheses of national importance.

c. The third and last way in which the substantive problem can emerge is at the direct instance of the consumer. For example, let us suppose that the policy people, who are prime among the intelligence consumers, are facing up to a revision of the established China policy. Let us assume that they summon some of the control and professional staff of intelligence to a meeting where the problem is put on the table. In the course of this meeting there will appear to be aspects of the China question which the policy people have not had to know about before. Let us assume that they have to do with population. A prospective change in policy has caused a substantive problem to emerge.

There is no real methodological problem in this case as presented. From the point of view of the intelligence organization, things have gone just as they should. To be sure, the assignment is so large and so general as to present serious difficulties, but in as much as intelligence was summoned to the meeting, intelligence may assume a good bit of further guidance from the consumers in precisely shaping the substantive problem to their needs. (This is stage 2 and will be discussed immediately.) But what happens all too often is that the decision to revise the policy is taken and discussion begun with intelligence not included. Weeks later, when the policy people are close against an immovable deadline, they discover they must have a new population estimate from intelligence and that at once. They raise a substantive problem all right, but they raise it to the consternation and despair of intelligence, which is asked to do a month's work over night.

2. Stage Two, the analysis of the substantive problem

The substantive problem has emerged in very rough form. Before the surveillance or research people can proceed with it they must give it some close and searching analysis. The aim of this analysis is not merely to discover and discard those elements which are irrelevant or unimportant, but more importantly, to shape the problem in such fashion that the solution (when it appears) will be directly applicable to the task of the consumers.

For example, the surveillance people have many possible courses of subsequent observation open to them by their discovery of Great Frusina's new missionary zeal. They can begin watching the church-state relationship looking for new angles; they can start an observation of the Great Frusina-Belgium relationship; they can skip over Great Frusina, Belgium, and the Congo, and start chasing after developments in the general field of missions to find new church policies therein. They are almost certain to turn up interesting leads no matter which of these, or other, lines they pursue. But that is not the question. The question is, what particular line of further observation is likely to prove of most importance to the security of the United States?

The research people who come back from the policy-on-China meeting may have much the same sort of choice to make. They were asked to come up with some population data; let us suppose that the original request was not more explicit than just that. Obviously there are dozens of kinds of population data only one or two of which will have any bearing whatsoever on the task of the policy people. What are these data, and in what degree of detail should they be worked up?

As the surveillance and the research people mull over

their substantive problems to find the most fruitful line of attack they will seek guidance. This guidance should come both from their own inner selves as they increase their understanding of their respective substantive problems and from the policy, planning, or operating people whom they are endeavoring to serve. Let me take the problem of guidance as it appears to the surveillance man.

He discovered that Great Frusina was enlarging its Christian missions program in the Congo; he knows that the Congo has large uranium deposits; he asks himself, is there a connection? When his foray into research reveals that Brother Nepomuk won a Nobel prize for work in geology he sees a connection and one aspect of *the most fruitful line of attack* has presented itself to him. He now has a hypothesis that Great Frusina is trying to get uranium from the Congo and that Brother Nepomuk is a Great Frusinan agent. At this point he must get outside guidance. What other lines of attack will the people whom he serves designate as fruitful, what do they propose to do about Great Frusina if such and such a line indicates an ill-intentioned activity on her part?

With the research people at work on the population of China the sequence may be exactly reversed. In their quest for direction they will promptly go back to the policy and ask their advice about lines of attack. They will also ask how the policy people see their task shaping up, and what their aim is in revising the old policy. If they get answers to their questions they can state the substantive problem in such a way that an answer to it will have practical utility to their principals. Moreover, as they advance into their research they will get useful hypotheses which spring from their familiarity with the subject matter, and which the policy people might never have got on their own.

But the methodological problem at issue is not that of inner guidance. It is that of guidance from without, guidance from the users of the knowledge which the intelligence people are trying to produce. It is one of the critical problems of the whole intelligence business and one to which I have devoted a substantial part of the next chapter. Suffice it to say here that the relationship between intelligence producers and intelligence consumers has been uneven; that intelligence often finds it impossible to get the sort of guidance which it must have to make its product useful; and that one of the places where this lack of guidance produces its most disastrous results is at this very stage 2 of the intelligence process. Unless the intelligence organization knows why it is at work, what use its product is to be designed to serve, and what sorts of action are contemplated with what sorts of implements, the analysis and proper formulation of the substantive problem suffer in proportion.

3. Stage Three, the collection of data

The collection of data is the most characteristic activity of the entire intelligence business. There can be no surveillance without the collection of data nor can there be research. Accordingly, an intelligence organization cannot exist until it does a broad and systematic job of collecting. But in this very task lie methodological problems which are so tough as to be almost unsolvable and in their unsolved state are a perpetual source of inefficiency.

a. Let me start with the easiest. This is the methodological problem which a member of the professional staff encounters when he embarks upon a piece of research. After he has blocked out his substantive problem, his next step is to see what data bearing upon the subject exist in his own and other intelligence organizations. Let us assume that his own files are in good shape and that his outfit has a centralized library of properly indexed documents. In a short time he can round up the materials which are in his own possession, so to speak. These materials indicate, as will also his horse sense, that there are other kindred materials in other neighboring intelligence organizations close by. He must reach these. I have already noted the difficulties in the task of reaching them if (1) he must communicate his wishes to another person in his own organization who has an exclusive mandate to collect data, and (2) if the other organizations possess no central library of indexed documents. The fact that intelligence organizations are likely to attempt to centralize the collecting function and are not likely to maintain a central index of their documents thus raises a considerable barrier to our researcher.

b. To proceed to a later step in this process, let us assume that the staff member discovers that even after canvassing every resource in his headquarters city there are still a number of unanswered substantive questions which he must explore. He must communicate with the field; he must try to explain to someone in a foreign capital what he wants to find out. Now if the man on the other end of the wire has formerly been a worker in the home office, if he has a feel for home-office functioning and personally knows the home staff, and if he is on his toes, he will the more readily understand what he is being asked to do and will do it with efficient good grace. He will grasp the instructions (which can be given in office shorthand) and will act pretty much as an overseas projection of the home staff. But if he has not served in the home office, and instead has gone to his foreign post improperly briefed on home problems then there may be difficulties.

The trouble begins with trying to explain in a letter or cable precisely what is desired, and in trying to explain it to someone starting from scratch. Requisitions for data of this sort must be spelled out in detail and to achieve results they must communicate in their substance a sense of urgency and importance. They are time-consuming. If they are no more than short blunt commands they are likely to be handled in a perfunctory fashion.

The trouble increases when the requisition deals with a subject to which the recipient is stranger. The home office may wish to have a foreign official interviewed on a technical demographic matter or wish to have someone audit and report on a scientific congress, but the men in the field may have had the wrong kind of professional training or no professional training at all, and thus be totally incompetent to handle the subject matter of the request. Or, most likely, the field staff is completely engulfed in making good on a previous request which seems to them to be of highest importance.

The above type of problem I have called the easiest of the problems of collection, because certain simple rules of good sense can probably beat it. But there are others which cannot be so easily disposed of. They are inherent in the surveillance phase of intelligence.

The surveillance force in a strategic intelligence operation is supposed in the first instance to watch actual, fancied, or potential ill-wishers or enemies of the United States and report on their activities. In the second instance the surveillance force is supposed to procure a less dramatic sort of information which is calculated to forward the success of our own policies. In certain aspects of both lines of work the surveillance force must work clandestinely. Or to put it another way: a surveillance force which was not equipped to work clandestinely could not deliver on a small but extremely important part of its task. Generally speaking, it could not deliver information which another country regarded as a secret of state. Many such secrets can be apprehended only by fancy methods which are themselves secrets of state. Thus a certain important fraction of the knowledge which intelligence must produce is collected through highly developed secret techniques. Herein begins perhaps the major methodological problem of the collection stage of the intelligence process.

It begins with the segregation of the clandestine force.

166

This segregation is dictated by the need for secrecy. An absolute minimum of people must know anything about the operation, and the greatest amount of caution and dissimulation must attend its every move. But unless this clandestine force watches sharply it can become its own worst enemy. For if it allows the mechanisms of security to cut it off from some of the most significant lines of guidance, it destroys its own reason for existence. This guidance, in the nature of things, should come from two sources: it should come from the ultimate consumers direct, or it should come from the ultimate consumer indirectly, through the overt part of the intelligence operation to which he (the consumer) has gone for help. As the relationship between the clandestine people and the direct and indirect consumers of their product is stopped down (as it may have to be for long periods); as it becomes formalized to the point where communication is by the written word only; as it loses the informality of man-to-man discussion, some of its most important tasks become practically impossible. Requisitions upon it for information become soulless commands which, through the innocence of the consumer, can take no notice of the capabilities of the organization. The consumer may ask for something the organization is not set up to deliver, or he may ask for so wide a range of information that the totality of resources of the organization would be fully deployed for months, or he may ask for something which though procurable is not worth the effort. With a high wall of impenetrable secrecy the consumer has great difficulty in not abusing the organization, and the organization has an equal difficulty in shaping itself along lines of greatest utility for the consumer. It is constantly in danger of collecting the wrong information and not collecting the right.

This danger is intensified by the very way clandestine intelligence works. Its job involves it in highly complicated techniques: the correct approach to a source, the "development" of source,[2] the protection of the source once it has been developed, the security and reliability of its own communications, and so on. Isolated by the security barrier, the perfecting of these techniques sometimes threatens to become an end in itself. One can understand the technician's absorbed interest in the tricks of his trade, but it is hard to pardon him when he gets his means and ends confused. There are cases on record where clandestine intelligence has exploited a difficult and less remunerative source while it has neglected to exploit an easy and more remunerative one. This kind of mis-collection would be far less likely to occur if the operation were not free to steer its own course behind the fog of its own security regulations.

4. Stage Four, the evaluation of data

If the language of intelligence were more precise it might use the word "criticism" in place of the word "evaluation," and if "criticism of data" were permitted we might move forward with a little more certainty and speed. The word criticism means the comparison of something new and unestablished with something older and better established. How does the new measure up to the old? The best critic, in these terms, is the man who has the greatest number of somethings on the established side of his ledger and the right sort of mind, for he will be able by direct or indirect comparison to appraise the validity of the new somethings as they come in. When he appraises in the direct method, viz., when he rejects a report which puts Great Frusina's steel capacity at 45 million tons be-

[2] For the meaning of the word "development" used in this sense see Richard Hirsch, *The Soviet Spies* (New York, 1947), esp. chap. 16. The people whom the Russians in Ottawa induced to betray their country did not betray it for money. They betrayed it because, through a subtle and persistent indoctrination, they became sure that in so doing they were benefiting humanity. There are many other ways of "developing" a source without the blunt use of the cash reward.

cause he knows from other evidence of unquestionable reliability that her capacity is 36 million tons, he may be said to have truthful information. When he appraises in the indirect method, viz., when he rejects a report which puts Great Frusina's harvester output at 30,000 per year because he cannot see what she could do with such a number, he is exercising what he hopes is good judgment.

In the research aspect of the intelligence business the collected data bearing on the substantive problem must of course be criticized before they can become the stuff from which a hypothesis emerges. If incorrect data are not rejected the emergent hypothesis will be accordingly incorrect, and the whole final picture incorrect. The methodological problem at issue boils down to a question of the expertise of the critic, the breadth of his understanding, and the freedom he is permitted in arriving at his appraisal of the data. Maybe, as in the case of an earlier problem, this one is as much a problem of administration as of methodology. But the point is, that the intelligence business in trying to run itself on an assembly-line basis and in trying to substitute administrative techniques for high-class professional personnel is all too likely to fall down on the all-important issue of the criticism of data. This is just another way of saying that we have lost too many scholars of knowledge and wisdom from a pursuit which cannot get along without them.

There is, however, a problem in the area of evaluation which can properly be called a methodological problem and one which is peculiar to the intelligence business. This problem arises because of the two ways in which the produce of the surveillance operation is distributed to the consumers. The first of these ways of distribution is through the finished digest or report or daily or weekly summary. The new stuff is put on the expert's desk; he criticizes it, judges its importance, mixes it with other data he received yesterday and the week before, gives it background and point, and sends it on to the consumer. This activity may be called "reporting," but as can be seen it contains all of the elements of research.

The second way in which the produce of the surveillance operation is distributed is in a much less finished form. The collectors pass to a sort of middleman what they have picked up. The middleman grades the data for reliability of source and accuracy and reliability of content, and may then distribute direct to the consumer or to the research staff of his own organization and to other intelligence organizations. The only ostensible reason for the existence of this middleman is that he is handling data which have been collected clandestinely. His organization must protect its sources. But the middleman—no matter how he came into existence—in actual fact does far more than obliterate the source's identity. He attempts to grade the reliability of the data. In doing so he is guided by some strange patterns of thought.

The middleman, according to standard practice, is restricted to a very narrow language in making his evaluations. He is permitted to grade the reliability of the source according to the letters A, B, C, D, and the content according to the numbers 1, 2, 3, 4. Thus A-1 would designate a report of unvarnished truth that was straight from the horse's mouth. Data from less dependable sources, and less accurate, might be B-2, C-4 etc. If the data happen to have come from a document, a newspaper or press release, or some such, one school of evaluators simply designates their value with the single word "documentary." Middlemen have insisted on not amplifying their comments beyond this elementary code and have done their best to see that others who might well be able to amplify were prohibited from doing so. They cling to this procedure on the ground that they are purveyors of a raw commodity and that it is their duty to distribute the commodity in the rawest state possible.

If this argument has any force the middlemen themselves do much to negate it. For they do not distribute the commodity in anything even approaching the raw state. They edit it, abbreviate it, translate it, and obscure its source if necessary. Worse, they frequently lose the point-of-observation—you might call it the slant of the information: Was it a French Communist, Socialist, or Rightist source which told the number of machine guns on the headquarters of the communist newspaper, *L'Humanité,* or which told of the new political instructions from the Vatican? When it lands on the consumer's desk, it is a semi-finished good.

Evaluation of the source may be a valid and valuable service of the middleman. If the source is known to be a good one and if it must be protected at all costs, to label it as grade A is helpful. But it is helpful and valid only in so far as the middleman knows what he is talking about, or in so far as the validity of the source has any bearing on the content. Often middlemen have no independent line on the reliability of the source, and instead of admitting as much will proceed to grade the source on the apparent reliability of the content. This movement in vicious circles is neither helpful nor valid.

Aside from the value of an authoritative evaluation of the source, there are within this procedure so many questionable elements that one scarcely knows where to begin. Actually one would not feel obliged to begin at all if these middlemen did not broadcast their product among people who are ultimate intelligence consumers and who tend to use the data without further and systematic criticism. But evaluated data do reach this group of consumers, and they are likely to accept the evaluation at face, and be accordingly misled.[3]

---

[3] Not to be forgotten is an equal peril. The busy consumer may not have time or inclination to read material put out in this form—in which case he remains innocent of the good along with the bad.

The first peculiar element consists of the middlemen themselves. Who are these people who neither themselves direct the clandestine operations nor sit in a place where they are forced to view *all* incoming materials? By all incoming materials I mean those collected overtly from open sources (newspapers, government reports, transcriptions of foreign radio broadcasts, etc.) as well as those collected clandestinely from other secret sources. Located where they are, the middlemen seem to be insulated from both the field experience of the operator and the desk experience of the research man who constantly and aggressively works at a specialty. I can understand how a man living in Rome and spending all his time collecting information on Italian politics can develop a high critical sense. I can understand how a research man in Washington who immerses himself in the data of his specialty and every moment of his professional life runs an obstacle race with his own and other people's hypotheses must have a high critical sense and a lot of critical ability. But I cannot understand how a man who passively reviews a wide range of material *without doing anything about it except grade it,* can have the necessary critical sense.

Another peculiar element of the evaluation business is closely akin to the last one. It is to be found in the implied assumption that the data of the social sciences have single non-relative values—that the datum, "Mr. Truman will try for the Democratic nomination in 1948," is in the same class with the datum, "All physical objects will fall sixteen feet in a perfect vacuum during the first second of their fall"—that if Mr. Hannegan gives the first datum it is the same thing as Dr. Millikan giving the second.

To illustrate further: During the war a document graded as A-3 was circulated which told of the American failure to take care of the inhabitants of the city of Oran, Algeria, in the winter of 1943. The source was given an A rating because it appeared to be someone familiar with the

172

situation; the content was graded as unreliable because the evaluator knew conditions in Oran were not as bad as represented. One recipient of this document who was well equipped for systematic criticism poked around until he identified the source as none other than an important French official and the document as the text of one of his off-the-record speeches. Now the official was unquestionably an A source on the matter, he should know from first-hand informants or even his own experience exactly what the situation was. But what he said about Oran under the Americans was of relatively little importance even if it had happened to be correct. The important aspect of this document was that violent adverse criticism of the Americans had come from an important man who was allegedly their friend and close ally. Its importance as a source on Oran was as nothing compared to its importance as a source on the ill-will, bad nature, or even mild perfidy of the official himself. One use of the document, in fact its real value, was completely obscured by the encoded evaluation. To serve the more important use, the evaluation should have called attention to the authorship of the document. If the document had fallen into the hands of American intelligence through the work of a secret agent whose indentity had to be protected, the evaluation would have required four or five sentences instead of one. But suppose that these sentences could not be written without compromising the agent, is this adequate reason for misleading the consumer through the A-3 evaluation? I would say not. I would say that if the middlemen could not think up some other method of handling the problem they should get out of the business.

The crowning peculiarity is the evaluation of a newspaper clipping by the use of the word documentary. What purpose this can serve has always eluded me. Furthermore, removing the name of the newspaper from the reproduction of the clipping is a positive disfavor to the recipient. Without it he is himself deprived of perhaps the most useful piece of information in making his own evaluation. For example, would you not like to know whether the *New York Times* or the *Daily Worker* was responsible for an estimate that Henry Wallace would poll ten million votes for President in 1948? Or would you settle for the attribution "documentary"? [4]

5. Stage Five, the moment of hypothesis

What is desired in the way of hypotheses, whenever they may occur, is quantity and quality. What is desired is a large number of possible interpretations of the data, a large number of inferences, or concepts, which are broadly based and productive of still other concepts.

There are two things an intelligence organization must have in order to generate more and better hypotheses: (1) professional staff of highest competence and devotion to the task, and (2) access to all relevant data.

There were many men who lived contemporaneously with Mahan and Mitchell, with Darwin and Freud, with Keynes and Pareto who could have made these men's discoveries, but who did not have the necessary training or quality of mind. But that these many others did not anticipate the great was not because they could not have had the necessary facts. To a very large extent the facts were there for anyone. The great discoveries of the race are the result of rigorous, agile, and profound thinking; the great discoverers have brains capable of such thinking and the stamina to face up to an intellectual responsibility. Great discoveries are not made by a lot of second-rate minds, no matter how they may be juxtaposed organizationally. Twenty men with a mental rating of 5 put together in one

---

[4] The official apology for this practice is that news items may be planted misinformation and that the evaluator does not wish to further the conspiracy. He thus uses the word "documentary" as a warning flag and as evidence that he is strictly neutral as far as interpretation goes. I am not impressed by this reasoning.

room will not produce the ideas of one man with a mental rating of 100. You cannot add minds as if they were so many fractional parts of genius. So long as the intelligence business behaves as if it could do this, it will not produce the sort of hypotheses essential to its mission.

But the intelligence business which recruited its professional staff from among the nation's most gifted people would not produce the good hypotheses unless these people had access to all the relevant data. This is by no means easy to arrange. Two things get in the way and the first of these is security.

Even though most of the subject matter of strategic intelligence falls in the field of the social sciences, it does not follow that the intelligence man has exactly the same problems as the university researcher or the journalist. He is dealing with state secrets upon which the safety or wellbeing of a nation may rest. On the theory that the degree of secrecy of a secret is a function of the number of people who know about it, a highly important secret cannot be too widely known. But a man cannot produce the good hypothesis in the matter of an important secret if he does not know as much as there is to know about it. It is interesting to speculate on how far Lord Keynes would have got if libraries withheld large blocks of economic data on the ground that they were operational, or how far Dr. Freud might have progressed if mental clinics sealed their records against him on the ground that they were too confidential. Yet intelligence people are constantly confronted with this very sort of argument. Security comes at a great cost in terms of results, and it should be allowed to interfere only so far as absolutely necessary. It must not be permitted as a cloak for inter-office and inter-departmental jealousies.

This matter of jealousies is the second of the two things that get in the way. I deal with it also at length in the next chapter. Here let me but say that, whatever the cause, one of the results is to withhold from intelligence one of the two prime ingredients of good hypotheses.

6. Last Stage, presentation

I am skipping the next-to-last stage (i.e. more collecting and more testing of hypotheses) in the intelligence process because it contains few, if any, problems not covered in stages 2 and 3. The last stage, the stage in which the established hypothesis is presented as a new and better approximation to truth, contains within it at least two important problems. These emerge from the form which the finished product must take. The most conspicuous aspects of this form is unadorned brevity and clarity.

To be sure, intelligence does produce long reports—some reach many hundred pages in length—but there are few studies or reports or monographs which do not also furnish the reader with the one- or two-page summary. In a way this is as it should be. The imposition of a word limit forces the intelligence producers to be clear in their thought and concise in their presentation, and it enables the hurried consumer to consume while he runs. But the result, while necessary, is by no means an unalloyed good. There is such a thing as a complicated idea; there is such a thing as so complicated an idea that it cannot be expounded in 250 words, or in two pie-charts, an assemblage of little men, little engines, and three-quarters of a little cotton bale. The consumer who insists that no idea is too complicated for the 300-word summary is doing himself no favor. He is requiring the impossible and is paying heavily for it. He is paying in two ways: he is kidding himself in his belief that he really knows something, and he is contributing to the demoralization of his intelligence outfit. The intelligence people who spend weeks of back-breaking work on a substantive problem and come up with an answer whose meaning lies in its refinements are injured at the distortion that may occur in a glib summary from which all real meaning has been squeezed. Next time they go at such a problem they will have less enthusiasm for exhaustive work, will turn in a poorer study with a still poorer summary tacked on the front. This is not a plea to the harassed consumer or man of action to read all the hundreds of pages of knowledge which come his way, but it is a plea for him to realize that there is a middle position and that as he lets it be known he will read nothing longer than one single-spaced page, a good many of his most loyal and hardest workers are going to lose some of their fervor in serving him.

A second problem of the presentation stage is the problem of footnote references. Intelligence consumers, unlike most serious and critical readers, have not demanded footnotes, in fact, they have often contemned footnoting as another evidence of the impracticality of the academic intelligence producer. The producer himself has his difficulties with the citation of sources. In those intelligence organizations where the rules of styling are made by men who do not understand the method of research there is the usual amount of lay opposition to the reference note. Again, even in organizations where the value of citing sources is fully understood, many sources must be concealed for the reason of security. Thus on both sides there are good and bad reasons for skimping on citations and citations are skimped.[5]

I know of no formula for evil that is any surer than sloppy research unfootnoted. Sloppy and footnoted is not good, but sloppy and unfootnoted multiplies the danger in

[5] Some organizations have developed a practice of citing as many open sources as the text requires and of citing secret or delicate sources in a code system. The consumer in these circumstances gets a better break even though some of the citations make no sense to him. If he must know the source for a given statement, he is always free to ask the producer for enlightenment. The producer, however, would seem to be the chief beneficiary. He has his record before him against the time when someone may challenge one of his statements, or he may have to revise or extend his study.

a way that the layman can hardly imagine. The following example is a case in point.

The military staffs of two countries, X and Y, had some pre-war conversations about the airfields which Y had in one of its colonies. Y told X that it had some airfields built, some about to be built on land already purchased, and a third group to be built when the land had been purchased. The outbreak of war turned the content of these conversations into an important item of intelligence, and one of Country X's intelligence outfits distributed a report which accurately named and located the fields and noted that some were ready, others not yet built, and others only planned. It cited its source and gave the dates of the conversations. So far so good.

A few months later another intelligence outfit in another country, Z, had occasion to get out a report on the colony. The report had a section on airfields. The information which it contained came from the earlier study, but it was changed in two respects: the matter of the land for those airfields whose land had not yet been bought was glossed over, and the citation of source was omitted. We now have a report which contains information on airfields in operation and another group soon to be completed.

A little later a second intelligence outfit of Country Z took the second report and entered the airfield data on cards. These cards were printed forms which had no appropriate box for noting that an airfield was in operation or in the process of construction. The cards carried no footnote references. All three categories of airfield thus dropped into category one. Taking information from the cards you would have thought that the area in question had fifty some more airfields than it in fact possessed.

It was about this time that a third intelligence outfit of Country Z came into being and inherited the card file of the second. It developed a technique of presenting airfield data on maps with symbols to indicate length and type of runway. Now back in the original document no length was given for the nonexistent runways of the fields to be, but it was noted that the areas to be purchased for airfield development were to be one mile square. This datum had been repeated in all the succeeding reports. But when the map-makers landed upon it they found it inconvenient. They did not wish to do the unrealistic thing of depicting a square runway one mile by one mile, so they compromised. They reasoned that the runways would be of maximum length, hence must follow the diagonal, and hence be something over a mile, say 7,000 feet, in length. This point decided, they made their maps and assigned a symbol indicating a 7,000 to 8,000 foot runway to the fields. As a matter of fact, later demonstrated, only one or two of the fifty-odd fields were ever completed.

This sort of error is by no means entirely ascribable to the lack of a footnote, but I would say that the lack of the footnote considerably enhanced its chances of occurring. Furthermore, the lack of the footnote made the correction of the original error more and more difficult as the data went through the producer-consumer-producer-consumer chain. By the time the map was made the discovery of the error demanded hours of the time of the most studious and professionally competent man who happened to have the hours to spend. And even so the damage was irreparable, for his more correct and cautious appraisal of the airfield situation in Y's colony could not possibly expect to reach all the consumers of the erroneous reports, or convince all those whom it did reach that his was the truer picture.

The methodological problems which I have discussed above would appear to be the most vexing ones. But my catalogue is not exhaustive. There are other problems and there are other facets to the ones already considered. Taken together they make the calling of intelligence a difficult one, and cause the results of the intelligence process often to fall below necessary standards of quality.

CHAPTER 11

PRODUCERS AND CONSUMERS OF INTELLIGENCE

THERE is no phase of the intelligence business which is more important than the proper relationship between intelligence itself and the people who use its product. Oddly enough, this relationship, which one would expect to establish itself automatically, does not do this. It is established as a result of a great deal of persistent conscious effort, and is likely to disappear when the effort is relaxed.

Proper relationship between intelligence producers and consumers is one of utmost delicacy. Intelligence must be close enough to policy, plans, and operations to have the greatest amount of guidance, and must not be so close that it loses its objectivity and integrity of judgment. To spell out the meaning of the last sentence is the task of the next pages.

The Problem of Guidance

One of the main propositions of this book may be summarized as follows: Unless the kind of knowledge here under discussion is complete, accurate, and timely, and unless it is applicable to a problem which is up or coming up, it is useless. In this proposition is recognized the fact that intelligence is not knowledge for knowledge's sake alone, but that intelligence is knowledge for the practical matter of taking action. Fulfillment of this function requires that the intelligence staff know a great deal about the issue which is under discussion in the other units of, say, the department charged with policy, plans, and operations, and that it have the largest amount of guidance and cooperation from them which can be afforded. The need for guidance is evident, for if the intelligence staff is sealed off from the world in which action is planned and carried out the knowledge which it produces will not fill the bill.

Let me be precise about the meaning of the word guidance. To be properly guided in a given task intelligence one must know almost all about it. If you wanted to find out from a road contractor how big a job it was to build a particular piece of road, you would not go to him and ask: "How hard is it to make a road?" Before you could expect any sort of meaningful answer you would have to stipulate what two points the road was to connect, what volume of traffic you wished to run over it, the axle loading of your heaviest vehicle, and so on. After you had made your specifications clear you still would have to wait for the final answer. The contractor might give a very rough estimate but refuse to commit himself until he had investigated the nature of the terrain to be traversed, the weather he would have to contend with while putting in the road, the local labor force, etc. When he had made these investigations he might come up with a figure for a road answering all the preliminary specifications but which was prohibitively high in cost. At this point he must return to you to begin conversations on compromises. Will you accept two lanes instead of three or four? Will you accept a more circuitous route with fewer cuts, fills, and difficult grades? Will you accept a less expensive surface? As you talk these matters over with him you find yourself, although you are not a professional road-builder, batting up suggestions as to how he can avoid this or that technical difficulty, and he, though no professional transportation man, begins asking you questions about your own problems. If things go well, you fetch your technical people in to the discussion, and he does also. Before you are done, your organization and his have got together straight across the board and a community of interest and understanding is developed that produces a workable plan and a smooth operation. You have naturally and unconsciously afforded him the guidance which was mandatory for his (and your) success.

Now this same sort of guidance is essential in the strategic intelligence business. Intelligence is not the formulator of objectives; it is not the drafter of policy; it is not the maker of plans; it is not the carrier out of operations. Intelligence is ancillary to these; to use the dreadful cliché, it performs a service function. Its job is to see that the doers are generally well-informed; its job is to stand behind them with the book opened at the right page, to call their attention to the stubborn fact they may be neglecting, and—at their request—to analyze alternative courses without indicating choice. Intelligence cannot serve if it does not know the doers' minds; it cannot serve if it has not their confidence; it cannot serve unless it can have the kind of guidance any professional man must have from his client. The uninitiated will be surprised to hear that the element of guidance which is present in the full at the lowest operational levels becomes rarer and rarer as the job of intelligence mounts in augustness.[1]

Without proper guidance and the confidence which goes with it, intelligence cannot produce the appropriate kind of knowledge. Its surveillance operation, while relatively certain to keep its eye on the obvious foreign problem areas, may well neglect the less obvious though significant ones. There will be a playing of hunches: "Watch Bolivia, they'll be screaming for information on it in a month"; "Isn't it about time we began watching for unrest in Madagascar or Soviet activities in India"; "Say, how about the Spanish underground, how about West African nationalism?" There will be plain and fancy guesswork on

[1] To see the intelligence-operations relationship at its best and most effective, one must clamber far down the administrative or command ladder. There, in the smallest units, the intelligence and the operations officer often exchange jobs—sometimes there is only one man for both jobs. In these circumstances there is no problem of guidance, and intelligence can be counted upon to do its job with a minimum of waste effort.

what is to be watched and what can be left to cool off. There will be differences of opinion as to what is and what is not important, and differences of opinion on where this, that, and the other matter belongs on the priority list. And whereas this striving to anticipate the trouble spot is not to be discouraged, it certainly should be supplemented continuously by the very best advice that the doers and intelligence consumers can offer.

The research aspect of intelligence suffers even more than the surveillance when improperly guided. In the first place the knowledge which it purveys may be inapplicable to the use it is supposed to serve, incomplete, inaccurate, and late. It is not reasonable to expect otherwise, for the kind of task intelligence is often asked to do in, say, a week's time or a day's time may be simply beyond human competence. To be able to deliver in the fashion apparently expected, and in the quality, would demand a research staff large enough to codify and keep up to date virtually the sum-total of universal knowledge. Even then it is doubtful if the result would be what was required unless intelligence had some advance warning of the next job.

In the second place, the want of sharp and timely guidance is chief contributor to the worst sickness which can afflict intelligence. This is the sickness of irresponsibility. Intelligence loses the desire to participate in the thing to be accomplished; it loses the drive to make exactly the right contribution to the united effort. It becomes satisfied with dishing up information without trying to find out what lies behind the order for them, without trying to make sense out of what appears senseless. When intelligent and sensitive men reach this stage they are no longer either intelligent or sensitive; they begin behaving as dumb and unhappy automatons who worry, if at all, about the wrong things. What they hand on in the way of knowledge is strictly non-additive; it must be worked over by someone else up the line, less well-informed than themselves, before it has value for the enterprise. And furthermore what they hand on is not only non-additive it may also be out of date or inadequate because long ago they quit caring.

There are a number of reasons why intelligence producers and consumers have difficulty in achieving the proper relationship. The first of these is a formal one and perhaps, on the surface at least, more typical of the armed services than the civilian departments.

The services are organized in the well-known staff pattern. At the highest level in the old War Department, for example, the Chief of Staff had under him a Deputy Chief of Staff, the General Staff, and the Special Staff. The General Staff still is composed of six divisions, each under the direction of a general officer. These are respectively responsible for matters concerning personnel, *intelligence,* organization and training, service-supply-procurement, plans and operations, and research and development. With modifications this pattern is easily recognizable in the top level of the other services, and typical of all services (again with modifications) in the descending order of their formations. For example, the commanding officer of an infantry division, a wing of combat aircraft, or a battleship would have a staff consisting of half a dozen officers, each of whom was entrusted with functions more or less accurately paralleling those of the Directors of the General Staff.[2]

The main job of all staffs is to keep the commander informed and assist him in making the "sound military decision." Each staff officer who is the specialist in his own particular function has the primary duty of contributing to his commander's understanding in that field, and a secondary duty to his fellow staff members. It is to be expected that the loyalties, as they jell in any human insti-

---

[2] It goes without saying that the research-and-development function is not usually represented at this level.

tution, will jell first and foremost along the vertical administrative line. That is, the people under the Director of Plans and Operations, say, will feel most loyalty to those who work next to them in the same small administrative unit and next most loyalty to the whole echelon of which they are a part, next most loyalty to the next echelon up, and so on to the Director himself. Until the loyalties of the people in the whole organization of Plans and Operations have traversed this vertical line, they will usually not spread out within the organization, and not until they have spread out within the organization will they start spreading over to other similar organizations (Intelligence or Personnel, for example) under the commander.

In these circumstances there is a formal reason inherent in staff structure why the Director of Intelligence might have his difficulties in getting from the other directors the kind of guidance on plans, projected operations, operational strength, etc., which he should have. The same reason might explain why the lower echelons of the several organizations find it hard to get together. But generalizing along this line is dangerous. Perhaps the only generalization which has validity is that rigorous staff structure increases the inertia of any large organization, and what seems to be true of the highest levels of the armed services is equally true of any very large commercial or industrial venture.

Some, basing their arguments upon a well-known phase of armed service doctrine, have held that inflexible relations across the main administrative lines are inherently more serious in the services than in big business. They point to the doctrine which is buried deep in one of the basic service formulae called "The Estimate of the Situation" [3] and assert that herein lies something which adds no

---

[3] This formula is designed primarily to fit an essentially military situation. Whereas the textbooks do not confine it to a tactical military situation there is a good bit more tactics involved than strategy. Furthermore,

small amount to the unsatisfactory relationship between intelligence producers and consumers.

The *estimate of the situation* is what a military commander must make before he decides upon a course of action.[4] Very briefly, the steps in the estimate involve first a knowledge of the environment in which the course of action is to be undertaken (terrain, hydrography, weather, etc.—in a grand strategical situation these factors would include the overall nature of the polity, economy, and society); secondly, a knowledge of the size, fighting strength, and disposition of the enemy forces (in a grand strategical situation this would amount to what I have termed strategic stature minus specific vulnerabilities); thirdly, a similar knowledge of the commander's own forces. From this knowledge the commander deduces the courses of action open to the enemy, and courses of action open to him which will accomplish, or further the accomplishment of, his mission. After he equates the enemy capability and possible courses of action against his own, he decides what his own course of action should be.

In the process briefly described above, the commander, of course has the services of his staff. Each of his staff officers has a clearly defined role in the procedure: personnel, operations, and logistics tells him precisely about his own force; intelligence tells him about the physical environment and the enemy force. The degree to which intelligence is permitted knowledge of his own forces and the courses of action which the commander may be mulling over are matters not spelled out in the formula. Since all

the strategy at issue seems to be a fairly straight military strategy. Nevertheless, the formula is applicable to what I have called the grand strategy, and top military men concerned with the grand strategy are not unlikely to think in its terms.

[4] Whether the commander actually prepares the estimate, or whether his chief of staff does, or whether his operations officer does, is likely to vary from circumstance to circumstance. Seldom if ever would the intelligence officer do it. In combat conditions the chief of staff or operations officer is the most likely candidate.

discussions of the estimate formula deal primarily with the responsibilities of the commander, the precise nature of what the intelligence officer should know and should not know about his commander's own forces is not specifically considered therein. Nor does it appear that formal study has been given the matter in other official service literature. It is perhaps unnecessary to say that a competent commander in a tense strategic or tactical situation would ordinarily desire to have his intelligence officer know everything which would contribute to his, the commander's, success. If he thought that an informed intelligence officer added another wise head to the staff he would ordinarily see that the latter were informed no matter what the doctrine might imply.

There is, however, one reason why the commander might wish to deny his G-2 (i.e. his intelligence officer) knowledge of his own forces. It can be, in fact it has been, argued that the G-2 should approach his job of estimating the enemy with complete objectivity, and that if he has full knowledge of his own forces and how they may be employed, his thought may jump ahead to the showdown of strength. If his mind does jump ahead, he will see his side about to win or lose, and his elation or fear will be reflected in his estimate of the enemy. If he sees his side the easy winner, the argument runs, he will tend to underrate the enemy; if the loser, to overrate the enemy. The commander who is going to have enough difficulties conquering his own subjective self may not wish to complicate the task by having to screen out that of his intelligence officer to boot. In these circumstances it is said, the commander may feel justified in keeping his intelligence arm in ignorance of his own plans and operational strength. But it seems to me that something is wrong with such a commander. If he counts on achieving an objectivity for himself it is hard to see why he should retain on his staff someone else whom he does not believe capable of such

187

objectivity. This point aside, it would appear to me that the doctrine at least allows the commander the option to tell intelligence nothing.

Whether or not he takes up the option would seem to depend upon the personal attributes of the commander, the magnitude of his command, the tenseness of the situation, and the need for air-tight security. One can conceive a wide range of possibilities beginning with a small unit action where the commander could not keep his intelligence officer in ignorance even if he thought it a good idea, and ending with the determination of a major strategic course of action at General Staff or Chief of Naval Operations level where considerations of time or security or something else might justify the commander in keeping his intelligence officer in the dark. At this level, too, the commander might tell everything to his G-2, but bind him to secrecy with respect to his (the G-2's) staff for the same reasons. It must be said, however, that no matter how good these reasons may appear to the commander, they can never seem so good nor so compelling to his intelligence officer.[5] The latter will always be miffed at the thought that his chief doubts his ability to overcome his subjective self, or that his chief holds him and his organization as a poor security risk. He will be a good deal more than miffed at the realization that no matter how hard he works, he will always run the risk of turning out a useless product.

Those who argue that the doctrine in the estimate-of-the-situation formula has within it the means of stultifying a free give and take between intelligence producers and

[5] The classic case of operational information withheld from intelligence is that of the atomic bomb. For months after its use, national intelligence at the highest level was expected to continue its speculative field (see Chapter 4) of work with little more knowledge of the bomb than the man in the street. That an analysis of Great Frusina's strategic stature should be meaningful, when the analysis was computed without reference to her specific vulnerability to the bomb, is something I have great difficulty in accepting.

consumers have a point. I would be more impressed with it if this doctrine were the only discernible cause, and if civilian departments which have inherited no such doctrine did not also have their difficulties in the producer-consumer relationship. There are other causes, and the doctrineless civilian departments fall victim to them along with the military.

The first of these may be called psychological. One of the sure ways to alienate a co-worker is to question his ability to add up a column of figures, take stock of a situation, or understand what he sees or reads. The vocabulary of insult and abuse about mental capacity is on a par with unsympathetic remarks about parenthood and ancestry, may be even ahead of them in provoking anger. On the theory that man's intellect alone separates him from other animals, perhaps this is understandable. Now, separating out from all the various steps necessary to accomplish an end, the thing called intelligence (intelligence in the context of this book) and bestowing it upon one group of men, to the formal exclusion of all others, is not to flatter the excluded. Deep in their subconscious selves they may well harbor the feeling that someone has told them they are not quite bright—that someone has in effect said, "Now don't you worry, your thinking is being done for you. We've arranged to relieve you of all thinking by giving you an external brain. We call it Intelligence. Whenever you want to know something, just go ask Intelligence." For many a man the separate existence of an intelligence arm must convey this sort of odious comparison.

If intelligence were staffed with supermen and geniuses who promptly and invariably came up with the correct and useful answer, the sting might wear off; intelligence might come to be revered by its users as a superior brain. But so long as intelligence is not so staffed, but in fact is staffed by men who, in the armed services at least, themselves often have small taste or special qualification for the work and do not intend to make it a life career, the relationship between producers and consumers will continue a troubled one.

A second cause for this state of affairs (and one which upon unfortunate occasions is closely related to the first), is what the language of intelligence would call the security reason. "Security" in this context, of course, means the *secrecy* with which certain affairs of state must be conducted.

As long as timing and surprise are essential aspects of policy and strategy there must be secrecy. A boxer who telegraphs his punches, a quarterback who inadvertently reveals the play, or a pitcher who cannot conceal the pitch is likely not to be the winner. The grand strategist—military or civilian—whose exact intentions and capabilities are known by the party of the second part finds himself without a strategy.

Policy makers and planners will, in the nature of things, deal with secrets of state, the disclosure of which would amount to a national calamity. (Although peacetime has its examples of what I am talking about, wartime provides those most readily understood: What if one month before the Allied assault on Normandy or the American landing at Leyte the enemy learned the exact time, place, and magnitude of the projected attack?) Likewise must the intelligence people have their secrets. A powerful intelligence organization can develop sources of information of a value utterly beyond price. They can be of such value that they themselves become the points of departure and the guarantors of success for a policy, a plan, or an operation. The revelation of such sources or even a hint of their identity will cause their extinction and perhaps the failure of the action based upon them. Their loss can be likened to the loss of an army or all the dollars involved in the Marshall Plan, or, upon occasions, the loss of the state itself.

The stakes being what they are, security and its formal

rules are an absolute essential. The first rule of security is to have the secret known by as few people as possible, and those of established discretion who, at the same time, must know the secret in order to do their share of the common task. What is the effect of this rule in the intelligence producer-consumer relationship?

When the rule is rigidly applied by the producers, the consumers are entitled to a legitimate doubt as to the validity of the producers' findings. Suppose you, as a planner, were told something which was contrary to all previous knowledge and belief and contrary to the laws of common sense? Would you accept it blindly and stake a policy or a plan upon it? What would be your emotions, your considered judgment, and your final decision if, after receiving such information, you went back to the producer to ask for confirming details and got a "Sorry, but I cannot say more than I put in the memorandum"?

Likewise, when the consumers—the policy people and planners—rigidly apply the rule, they give the intelligence producers good cause for non-compliance; or the production of useless knowledge. Suppose you were an intelligence producer and suppose one of your consumers appeared with a request for everything you could find out about Java. Suppose the request were phrased just this way. Suppose your entire staff were occupied on other high-priority jobs and that you could not put any of them on his request without some justification on his part. Suppose you told him this. It might be that he would feel he could not give you the justification without a breach of security. You are at cross-purposes. In some cases the consumer would drop the matter there. But in others, he would go back to his office, carry his request up through two echelons of his own organization, and see that it came down to you through two echelons of yours. You would be given your orders to get to work on Java.

The chances are excellent that a request which comes

through in this fashion is a request in which the security issue is paramount. The consumer does not really want to know all about Java; he wants to know merely about some tiny fraction of it. But he dares not stipulate the fraction for fear of revealing his intent. So he asks for all of it, hoping to get his information out of one paragraph or chapter of your encyclopedia. He has no guarantee that this paragraph or chapter is not the very one you consider unimportant and accordingly will leave out. Nor have you any guarantee that if you write the paragraph or chapter you will write it in the way that will serve his interests best.

Now what I have said above is the extreme case. When the issues are of highest importance both producers and consumers go to all permissible lengths to help each other forward the success of the common task. But this very leaning over backwards merely confirms the existence of the basic problem which security throws in the way of a perfect relationship. Furthermore, when the substantive issue is of some lower order of importance no one may lean over backwards and something akin to the impasse I have described can easily develop.[6]

[6] The security problem within a single military department occasions some of the difficulties I have enumerated in my extreme case. But it occasions worse ones in the relationship between the military and civilian departments. For very good reason some, if not all, civilian departments have poor reputations for safeguarding secrets of state. They have been slack in their investigations of dubious personnel; they have talked when silence was in order. They have been responsible for outrageous leaks. In these circumstances, officers of the services who have been thoroughly indoctrinated in the necessities for security are understandably reluctant to open their hearts to the civilians. Moreover, these officers, who face direct and severe penalties if they themselves are responsible for a leak, fully realize that no such penalties are imposable upon civilian employees. Without an official secrets act such as the British have, a loose-talking civilian or a man under the influence of a foreign power will in most cases suffer no greater harm than dismissal from his job.

By the above I do not mean to imply that all people wearing the uniform are reliable and those in civvies not. I do mean to say that the military's record for safeguarding secrets is better than the civilians, and that this fact plus differences in applicable penalties aggravates the security problem in the service-civilian relationship.

What I am concerned with in these paragraphs is not to play down the importance of security regulations and their observance. I am concerned with the point that security is like armor. You can pile on the armor until the man inside is absolutely safe and absolutely useless. Both producers and consumers of intelligence have their secrets, and in safeguarding them they can so insulate themselves that they are unable to serve their reasons for being. This problem is so critical to intelligence that it deserves the continuing study of a high-powered board. It cannot be met by the earnest but informal and sporadic efforts which are current today. Nor do I believe it would vanish with the passage of an official secrets act. Such an act would help enormously, but it would not be the all-powerful panacea its proponents would have it.[7]

A last reason for the misunderstandings between intelligence producers and consumers is an understandable reluctance on the part of consumers to embark upon a hazardous task on the basis of someone else's say-so. After all, if anyone is going to be hurt it probably will not be the producers. I will warrant that the Light Brigade's G-2 was high on the list of survivors in the charge at Balaclava. So it will be in less dramatic instances. The casualties, in both the literal and figurative senses, will be to the intelligence users first, and to the producers late down the line. In these circumstances it is easy for the users to adopt the attitude expressed in the rhetorical question: "Why should

[7] If such a law existed, it could do no more than provide penalties for the unathorized disclosure of state secrets. Penalties have been deterrents to crime, but no matter how severe, penalties have not obviated crime. There will always be people to whom the penalty is a secondary consideration. Some would choose to disclose state secrets of a given order of importance even though the penalty were death. In these terms is it reasonable to suppose that secrets of this order of importance can be any more tightly held than at present? I would say that an official secrets act would have little if any effect upon the intelligence producer-consumer relationship where the substantive issue was one of top national importance and hence highest secrecy.

intelligence worry about doing a perfect job, after all it's not their neck?" From this there can emerge a feeling of disrespect, perhaps even of derogation, for the word of those who do not carry the weight of operational responsibility. Let intelligence make any kind of mistake for which there is a natural penalty, and the relations between the two are likely to worsen.

One last word: intelligence is bound to make mistakes. Some of the questions it is required to answer demand a divine omniscience; others demand more painstaking work than can be accomplished in the time allotment; still others can be had only with the most elaborate sort of undercover preparations which have never been made. But let intelligence make a mistake or come up with an inadequate answer and all too often the reaction of the consumers is on the uncomprehending and bitter side: "I wouldn't ask those geniuses to tell me how many pints there were in a quart." When intelligence errs there seems to be less tolerance of its error than there is for the error of other mistaken specialists. For example, when a dentist pulls out the wrong tooth (as the best dentists have done) or a lawyer loses a case, the client's reaction is not that he, himself could have done a better job, and that henceforth he will do his own dental and legal work. Yet in intelligence matters, pardonably wrong diagnosis and understandably inadequate presentation very often do arouse just such a reaction in the client. For good reason or bad, an intelligence failure seems to rankle out of proportion to its importance, and to tend to justify the consumer in doing his own intelligence henceforth.

Thus there are a number of reasons why the relationship between producers and users may at times be extraordinarily difficult with the result that the all-important element of guidance is lost. Once this occurs, intelligence must remain innocent of the consumers' requirements, and

194

the consumers innocent of intelligence's capacity to contribute to their problems.[8] In wartime the closer to the fighting front and the smaller the operating unit, the better the relationship and the keener the guidance; the more remote from the fighting front and the larger the unit, the worse the guidance. In peacetime there are few situations comparable to the fighting front. Where they do exist they do not possess that element of common physical peril which makes all men of one side friends and brothers. In peacetime top-level intelligence must function in the very area where wartime relations were worst and where without the leaven of what you might call front-line tolerance they are likely to remain worst. One concludes that of the two dangers—that of intelligence being too far from the users and that of being too close—the greater danger is the one of being too far. But what of the other?

The Problem of Objectivity and Integrity

The other danger—that of being too close to the consumers—is, however, not to be readily dismissed. In a moment of intense exasperation, intelligence producers and consumers might agree that the administrative barriers between them should be knocked down and that intelligence should be moved piecemeal into the policy section or the plans section or operations section, or that intelligence should be broken up into its regional and functional units and dispersed among appropriate parts of the total organization. If this were done, intelligence

[8] During the war there was a very interesting parallel in the relationship between certain civilian scientists in enterprises under control of the government, and the military men they were serving. As civilians the scientists had few natural insights into the detailed requirements of the military and spent no small amount of time trying to find these out. The military, on the other hand, lacked a similar natural insight into the capabilities of modern science. There was thus a wall between them which had to be demolished before the scientists could get the right kind of guidance, and before the military could gain the proper knowledge of what they might ask the scientists to work on.

would very likely acquire all the guidance it could possibly ask for—perhaps even more than it could legitimately stomach. There will be great and obvious advantages; there will also be costs, some of them considerable. Let us begin with the meanest.

Intelligence is likely to be diverted from its essential task. I mean this in its most crude sense: the intelligence personnel who are professionally studious and also possessed of some of the talents of the doer are going to find themselves asked to share the non-intelligence burden of the office. Personnel raids of this sort are very familiar to intelligence people everywhere; practically everyone not in intelligence has a way of fancying the best of intelligence staff as a pool of unencumbered and elite manpower ready to be tapped at will. Fighting off such raids is a well-known necessity. In the context under discussion resistance is likely to be useless and once the intelligence man has crossed the line, into operations, say, he is going to have greatest difficulty arranging his return to intelligence. Generally speaking, once out of the intelligence phase of the work he will be engulfed in the day-to-day business of the new job. Soon the intelligence staff is whittled down to its least valuable members, which is to say intelligence has lost its identity and its functioning integrity. This very thing has happened enough times to be worthy of serious consideration.

Secondly, intelligence, if brought too close to its consumers, is likely to be diverted in a slightly less crude sense, but scarcely a less damaging one. For instance, the detailed problems of an operating office can be many and compelling. A great many of them require an "Ask Mr. Foster" type of research. The tendency will be to put intelligence staff on this kind of work. This is not to argue the work's unimportance, but it is to argue that absorbing too much intelligence talent in it is to make poor use of intelligence. Intelligence should have long stretches of uninterrupted time to carry out long-range projects which can be done in no other circumstances.

Thirdly—and this would be true only where intelligence was not only brought across the line administratively, but also broken up and dispersed among appropriate planning or operations sections—the substantive integrity can be seriously injured. In an earlier chapter I indicated how intelligence can handle surveillance and research problems which cut across its regional or functional lines. According to this method a problem such as Spanish influence in Argentina would become the charge of an *ad hoc* committee under the supervision of a project leader (either a Spanish or Latin American expert) and under the ultimate management of the staff I called the Control Staff. In such a way one may be relatively sure that the totality of resources which intelligence can turn to the problem are turned to it. But when the intelligence organization has been fractioned and spatially separated and put into closest contact with the consumers, no such method need be followed. Indeed it is easy to see how a Spanish unit chief would call up one of his intelligence men, ask what he could find out about Spanish doings in Argentina, and lay no prohibition upon him against going to another building to talk with his Latin American opposite number. It is not merely possible, it is highly probable, that the multitude of problems of this sort would be dealt with by people who are expert in only one sector of the subject.

Nor is this, and the want of substantive give and take which it implies, the only disadvantage. In addition there is the matter of contrasting standards of performance as a price of dispersal. An intelligence outfit, which is administratively separated from its consumers and unified within itself, is able to strive for a uniformly excellent product. The best work passing through Control will inevitably become the scale against which other work is measured. Destroy the centralization and the unity and you destroy the best and most natural method of establishing competition and of deriving good from it.

To all the foregoing, there may be devisable administrative remedies. I doubt if the remedies will be wholly effective, but they may be able to meet the worst objections. There is, however, one high-order disadvantage in bringing the producers and consumers of intelligence too close together which will elude the most ingenious of administrative devices: *this is the disadvantage of getting intelligence too close to policy.*

This does not necessarily mean officially-accepted high United States policy, but something far less exalted. What I am talking of is often expressed by the words "slant," "line," "position," and "view." Almost any man or group of men confronted with the duty of getting something planned or getting something done will sooner or later hit upon what they consider a single most desirable course of action. Usually it is sooner; sometimes, under duress, it is a snap judgment off the top of the head. The way in which such people arrive at this most desirable course of action does not require them to examine all the facts critically and dispassionately and to arrange them into a logically sound and secure pattern. They may arrive at their solution in ignorance of many relevant and important facts, and with their prejudices and clichés of thought discriminating in favor of the facts which they do use. This kind of off-the-cuff solution tends to harden into what I have termed policy—in the unexalted sense of the word. Their "view" is thus and so; their "position," therefore, thus and so; their "line," in support of the "view" and "position" thus and so. Add the ingredients of time and opposition and you have something which can be called "policy" without doing too much violence to the language. Even though this policy may be arrived at by rule of thumb, hazard, or blind intuition, it does not follow that it is invariably and necessarily wrong. Sometimes it is inspirationally perfect. But my point for the moment is that unless the necessity for action is too pressing to permit impartial analysis of all the available facts, preferably before "view" jells into "position," but in any event antecedent to action, this procedure is full of unnecessary risks. If there is an intelligence staff on the periphery it should be instructed to do the systematic analysis.

Now an intelligence staff which must strive for reasoned and impartial analysis, if it is to strive for anything, has its own difficulties with view, position, slant, and line. After all, it is made up of men whose patterns of thought are likely to color their hypotheses and whose colored hypotheses are likely to make one conclusion more attractive than the evidence warrants. The main difference between professional scholars or intelligence officers on the one hand, and all other people on the other hand, is that the former are supposed to have had more training in the techniques of guarding against their own intellectual frailties. Policing their inescapable irrationalities is a twenty-four-hours-per-day task. Even so, they are by no means always successful. The history of intelligence is full of battles between the pro-Mihailovitch and pro-Tito factions, between the champions and opponents of aid to China, between defenders and detractors of the Jewish national home in Palestine. The fact that there have been such differences of opinion among supposedly objective and impartial students who have had access to substantially the same material, is evidence of someone's surrender to his irrational self. These differences of opinion have appeared among intelligence organizations which were administratively separate from the people they were to serve.

If intelligence under the best of conditions finds itself guilty of hasty and unsound conclusion, is it likely to find itself doing more of this sort of thing when it is under the administrative control of its consumers in plans or operations? My answer is, yes. I do not see how, in terms of human nature, it can be otherwise. I do not see how intelligence can escape, every once in so often, from swinging into line behind the policy of the employing unit and prostituting itself in the production of what the Nazis used to call *kämpfende Wissenschaft*.[9] Nor do I see how, if the unexpected occurred, and intelligence invariably came up with findings at variance with the policy of the employing unit, intelligence could expect to draw its pay over an indefinite period. I cannot escape the belief that under the circumstances outlined, intelligence will find itself right in the middle of policy, and that upon occasions it will be the unabashed apologist for a given policy rather than its impartial and objective analyst. As Walter Lippmann sagely remarks, "The only institutional safeguard [for impartial and objective analysis] is to separate as absolutely as it is possible to do so the staff which executes from the staff which investigates. The two should be parallel but quite distinct bodies of men, recruited differently, paid if possible from separate funds, responsible to different heads, intrinsically uninterested in each other's personal success."[10]

For these reasons, what is unquestionably gained in *guidance* may well be lost in the *integrity* and *objectivity* of the operation. The absorption of intelligence producers by the intelligence consumers may prove to be too heroic a cure for both disease and patient.

The only way out of the dilemma seems to me to lie in the very compromise that is usually attempted: guarantee intelligence its administrative and substantive integrity by keeping it separate from its consumers; keep trying every

[9] To be rendered roughly as "knowledge to further aims of state policy" —the kind of "knowledge" put forth by the party "intellectuals" purporting objectively to prove such phenomena as Aryan Supremacy, German Destiny, the need for *Lebensraum*, the Judeo-Capitalistic-Bolshevist Encirclement, the Stab in the Back, the *Versailles Diktat*, etc.

[10] Quoted from *Public Opinion* (The Macmillan Co., N.Y., 1922) with the kind permission of the publisher. Chap XXVI § 2.

known device to make the users familiar with the producers' organization, and the producers with the users'
organization.

The Problem of Intelligence and Policy Formulation

What has just been said of intelligence and policy is not
all that must be said. Certainly intelligence must not be
the apologist for policy, but this does not mean that intelligence has no role in policy formulation. Intelligence's
role is definite and simple. Its job might be described in
two stages: (1) the exhaustive examination of the situation
for which a policy is required, and (2) the objective and
impartial exploration of all the alternative solutions which
the policy problem offers.

It goes without saying that intelligence can skew its
findings in either stage, especially in the second, so that
one alternative will appear many times more attractive
than the others. It is not heartening to reflect that just this
has been done, though it would be hard to prove that
every such crime was one upon which intelligence em-
barked entirely on its own responsibility. For instance,
during the war some British intelligence organizations
could prove at the drop of a hat that there was such a
thing as a soft underbelly and that compared to it all other
portals to fortress Europa were as granite. Merely because
intelligence is capable of getting off the beam is not sufficient reason to exclude it entirely from policy considerations or to contemn it as unprincipled. As long as its
complement of professional personnel is of high intellectual and moral caliber, the risks which the policy-making
users run in accepting its analysis of alternatives are far less
than those they would run if they excluded intelligence
from their councils.

The Problem of Intelligence (the Product) and its Acceptance

As far as an intelligence staff is concerned, what it desires above all else is that its findings prove useful in the making of decisions. There is, however, no universal law which obliges policy, plans, and operations to accept and use these findings. If intelligence is guilty of poor method or errors in judgment, there is nothing to coerce its putative consumers into acting upon its advice. This fact has its benefits and its evils. The benefits are almost too obvious to mention: for example, no one would advocate taking a course of action which evidence, not considered by intelligence, indicated to be suicidal. Just because an intelligence aberration happens to indicate the law of gravity is inoperative in Lent does not constitute sufficient reason to jump off a high roof on Good Friday. But in this very laudable liberty to discount intelligence lies a source of danger. Where is one to start discounting and where stop discounting intelligence?

In one of the books for children written by James Willard Shultz there is a story of some Indian tribes readying themselves for the warpath. The combined chiefs met to discuss the projected operation and instructed the headquarters G-2 (a medicine man named White Antelope) to give them an estimate of enemy capabilities. In a couple of days' time White Antelope, having gone through the necessary professional gyrations, came back to the combined chiefs with his estimate. It seems that the gods had favored his ceremonial by granting him a vision in which he saw a lone raven seated on the carcass of a dead deer. As the raven feasted he did not notice a magpie who slipped into a tree overhead and took some observations, nor did he notice that the magpie gave the signal for the concentration of his deployed force. When the magpies' build-up in strength was sufficient, they dropped down

upon the raven and attacked. The raven put up a game
fight, but as things moved from bad to worse decided to
retreat to prepared positions. If White Antelope were an
irresponsible G-2 he might have left it at that, but being
a responsible man and feeling that he should make his
contribution to the common cause, he hazarded an interpretation. To him the raven was the allied force and the
magpies were the enemy—the facts would justify such an
interpretation—and plainly the enemy's capabilities were
more than adequate. The allies were in for a licking. He
said as much. But Bull Head who was supreme commander spoke up and said in effect, "What you tell us is
not much more than that the expeditionary force will be
in danger. This we already know. As to the raven and
the magpies, it is my belief that we are the magpies, and
the enemy, the raven. We start tomorrow." The G-2's
estimate had not been accepted.

It is important to notice that White Antelope had done
the best he knew how and according to a method which
was standard operating procedure. Bull Head himself
would have admitted as much. Bull Head did not override his G-2 because of a reasoned distrust of his data or
a rational doubt of his objectivity; he overrode him on the
basis of a hunch and probably a wishful one at that.

Now I do not wish to be the one who rejects all hunches
and intuitions as uniformly perilous, for there are hunches
based upon knowledge and understanding which are the
stuff of highest truth. What I do wish to reject is intuition
based upon nothing and which takes off from the wish.
The intelligence consumer who has been close to the problem of the producer, who knows it inside out, may have
an insight denied the producer. His near view of the
broad aspects of the problem and his remoteness from the
fogging detail and drudgery of the surveillance or research
may be the very thing which permits him to arrive at a
more accurate synthesis of what the truth is than that

afforded the producer. But let the consumer, in these circumstances, beware. If he overrides the conclusions of his intelligence arm, and makes a correct estimate, let him deeply ponder why this came about. Let him not get the notion that he need only consult his stars to outdo his G-2. If he does get that notion, he will destroy his intelligence organization—its members will not seek truth so that a soothsayer may negate their conclusions and embark upon a perilous course. If there is anything in the rational philosophy of the West—which holds that the mind is the best long-run solver of unknowns—the consumer who derides the philosophy runs great risk of making a series of climactic errors. From these there may be no second chance.

Adolf Hitler was such an intelligence consumer. There is every reason to think that his intelligence at the technical levels of both surveillance and research was adequate. In fact there is reason to think it was a good deal better than that. There is every reason to think that his general staff was technically competent. There is every reason to believe that he did not get inaccurate knowledge from his intelligence or poor advice from the staff which based its judgments upon this knowledge. Hitler had his hunches and the first few of them were brilliant. Because of luck, or because of a profound and perhaps subconscious knowledge of the situations at issue, he called the turn correctly and in opposition to his more formal sources of advice. But the trouble was that he apparently did not try to analyze the why of his successful intuition. He went on as if his intuition were a natural, personal, and infallible source of truth. When he began to reap the natural penalties for such errors as overestimating the Luftwaffe's capabilities in Britain and underestimating the capabilities of the Soviet Union, when he ordered a cut-back in German war production in the fall of 1941 because he thought the war was won, he not only took some of the direct and positive steps to lose the war, but he also took an indirect and equally hurtful one in that he damaged severely the utility of his staff and intelligence services.[11]

When intelligence producers realize that there is no sense in forwarding to a consumer knowledge which does not correspond to preconceptions, then intelligence is through. At this point there is no intelligence and the consumer is out on his own with no more to guide him than the indications of the tea leaf and the crystal ball. He may do well with them, but for the long haul I would

[11] The following is illustrative, and I have no doubt that similar incidents occurred outside the Third Reich: Shortly after Mr. Roosevelt's message to Congress (6 January 1942) in which he put our airplane and tank production goals at seemingly astronomical figures (we were to produce 45,000 tanks during the year) Ribbentrop, who moved in highest Nazi circles, telephoned the Foreign Office's chief negotiator and advisor on economic matters—a man named Ritter. The question in Ribbentrop's mind was, of course, the bluff and propaganda quanta in the President's figures. He already had decided (out of intuition, perhaps) that the goals which Mr. Roosevelt had mentioned were very largely nonsense. What he asked Ritter was an estimate of American steel capacity.

Ritter replied that the last firm figure available on actual production was 45,000,000 tons and that the consensus placed capacity at 57,000,000. He may have talked in the familiar way of the expert, and instead of using the word "million" merely used the numbers forty-five and fifty-seven. A few days later—after hearing that some other experts had revised the figure upwards to 110,000,000 tons Ribbentrop called him again and scolded him for what he felt to be an over-inflated picture. Ritter, making clear his own position, asserted that in his judgment the figure 110,000,000 was too high and that his own estimate was somewhere between 60 and 70 million tons.

In another few days Ribbentrop was back again. This time with a note of triumph in his voice, he put the question, "Do you think the 45,000 tank figure is possible?" The answer: "Yes I think it is possible." The next query: "But if you accept the tank figure and each tank contains at least two tons of steel, already you have accounted for 90,000 tons of steel. Your estimated overall steel capacity would be completely absorbed in tanks." The reply: "But Mr. Minister, you are talking in terms of thousands of tons. We speak of steel production in terms of millions." Ribbentrop hung up abruptly.

It was within Ribbentrop's province to question the estimate of the experts, and the fact that his technical ignorance was profound seems in no way to have inhibited him. Indeed, in other circumstances one can easily imagine a difference between consumer's hunch and the producer's estimate which did not provoke a final and clarifying telephone call. In these circumstances a course of action might be adopted which was close to pure folly. (I am indebted to Professor Harold C. Deutsch for this anecdote.)

place my money elsewhere. Without discarding intuition as invariably a false friend, I would urge the consumer to use it with a full knowledge of its frailties. When the findings of the intelligence arm are regularly ignored by the consumer, and this because of consumer intuition, he should recognize that he is turning his back on the two instruments by which western man has, since Aristotle, steadily enlarged his horizon of knowledge—the instruments of reason and scientific method.

APPENDIX

APPENDIX

KINDS OF INTELLIGENCE

INTELLIGENCE at the national level in both wartime and peacetime has a great number of separate and distinct forms, and is carried out by a wide range of federal departments and agencies.[1] Until the general reader is aware of the multiplicity of forms, and aware of the rough pattern of their arrangement, his elementary confusion is easily justified. .

In the pages which follow, I have three aims: First and foremost, to set out in an orderly, if somewhat arbitrary, form the main kinds of intelligence in which our federal government engages. This I will do in the charts and explanatory text. Secondly, I will indicate the particular kinds of intelligence with which this book has been concerned. And lastly, having given an oversimplified picture, I will endeavor to reintroduce a corrective element of murkiness and confusion in so far as this is characteristic of the federal intelligence pattern.

EXPLANATION OF THE TERMINOLOGY OF THE CHARTS

1. SECURITY AND POSITIVE INTELLIGENCE

a. *Security Intelligence.* To put it in its simplest terms, you should think of security intelligence as basically the intelligence behind the police function. Its job is to protect the nation and its members from malefactors who are working to our national or individual hurt. In one of its most dramatic forms it is the intelligence which continuously is trying to put the finger on the clandestine agents sent here by foreign powers. In another, it is the activity which protects our frontiers against other undesirable gatecrashers: illegal entrants, smugglers, dope runners, and so

---

[1] See diagrams following p. 210.

on. It identifies our own home-grown traitors and persons violating the federal law. By and large, security intelligence is the knowledge and the activity which our defensive police forces must have before they take specific action against the individual ill-wisher or ill-doer.

b. *Positive Intelligence.* Positive intelligence is harder to define. If one wished to talk in not-quite-true riddles, he might say that positive intelligence was what was left of the entire field after security intelligence had been subtracted. This is a starter, but not too helpful.

To approach it more directly: it is all the things you should know in advance of initiating a course of action. Thus, positive military intelligence in anticipation of an offensive operation furnishes the military commander with all knowledge possible on the strength and deployment of the enemy and on the physical attributes of the battlefield to be. The idea is that the commander should know what he will be up against before he goes into battle. There are many other kinds of positive intelligence besides military, but all of them have about them the *preparatory* characteristic typical of this phase of military intelligence.

If this were the only aspect of positive intelligence, the defining of it would not be so difficult. But there is another aspect, and one which is closely enough akin to security intelligence to cause some trouble. Everyone who knows that there is such a thing as positive military intelligence knows that it does not confine itself to furnishing strategists, planners, and field commanders with the sort of knowledge they must have before they take action. Practically everyone knows that military intelligence must also try to find out what the enemy's plans are, so that he (the enemy) will not be able to take one's own forces by surprise. In other words, positive intelligence is not merely an intelligence for the commander on the offensive (the man who has taken or plans to take the initiative), it is also the intelligence which protects this commander against the surprise moves of his opponent. In this aspect it has an important defensive and protective flavor. Is this flavor distinguishable from what I have given security intelligence? The answer is, yes.

Let me illustrate the distinction. A policeman, alerted by security intelligence, will protect your house against burglars, or, if the house is robbed, he will use security intelligence to catch the burglars. But this policeman will not warn you when there is to be a boost in the price of beef, nor will he tell you when your bank is going to fail. This is not his job. To get this kind of protective knowledge, you will have to patronize some sort of positive intelligence service.

2. FOREIGN AND DOMESTIC

"Foreign" and "domestic" in the context of intelligence refer to the targets of intelligence, not to the place where the intelligence activity takes place. For example, by "security intelligence—foreign," I mean the security intelligence which applies itself to another country's spies, saboteurs, or *agents provocateurs;* which identifies foreign narcotic and smuggling rings. By "positive intelligence—foreign," I mean knowledge of other countries and other people, and, incidentally, what those countries may be hatching in the way of policy or action against our national interest.

By "security and positive intelligence—domestic," I mean that kind of intelligence which deals exclusively with people and problems local to the United States, its territories, and possessions.

3. LONG-RANGE, MEDIUM-RANGE, SHORT-RANGE

There are many possible levels of intelligence. One knows, for instance, that there is in all probability an intelligence project or two designed for members of the cabinet which has high Soviet policy as a subject; that there is another intelligence which keeps the State Department informed about political goings-on in, say, Iran or Italy; and that there is still another intelligence which informs an individual officer of the State Department exactly what tone he should strike in a note to, say, the Danish Ambassador in Washington. One feels instinctively that there are several "intelligences" or several levels of intelligence, which indeed there are. In military formations, there is usually an intelligence organization at each staff or command echelon. When in wartime one started at the Joint Intelligence Committee at Joint Chiefs of Staff level and progressed down any of the various service ladders to the intelligence section of the smallest ground, naval, or air unit, one touched perhaps as many as fifteen levels. As one descended, the intelligence function became more and more restricted, and more and more technical. But in a diagram such as I have given, or in a book such as this, there is no point in too fine a breakdown in the "function to be served."

4. FUNCTION TO BE SERVED

What has already been said in the section on Range may be extended to explain this column in the charts. The point is that the federal government has a great many levels of responsibility and, in general, a level of intelligence to serve each one of them. Its top responsibility is to the security of the national state against internal and external enemies. This I have called the long-range intelligence of high policy, the national security, the national welfare, and the grand strategy. This intelligence is the intelligence of *national survival*.

Immediately below, I have put the intelligence of departmental *policy*. By this—and I have called it medium range—I mean the kind of knowledge (and the activity which produces it) which is necessary for the State Department, the Army Department, the Navy Department, and the Air Force Department to have in carrying out their specific functions. Granted that it is difficult, perhaps impossible, to identify a departmental problem which has no supra-departmental significance, at the same time it must also be granted that there are technical departmental problems which have far less of this significance than others.

The least function which I have entered on the diagram is the function of departmental *operations*. This is, in my "positive foreign" category, what I have called short range.

Let me illustrate all three levels from a subject of current interest: our arming of the Latin American republics. Intelligence for the basic decision to make standard U.S. military equipment available to the Good Neighborhood should be furnished by the highest level. This intelligence deals with the world situation, the strategic stature of other countries, and the courses of action open to them. It tries to estimate how the world situation will be altered by our decision and whether to our advantage or not.

Suppose, now, that on the basis of top-level intelligence our high policy people decide that we should work to standardize military equipment in Latin America. At once several government departments will have their own policy problems to straighten out. The State Department may have been having its troubles with Cuba, or Chile, or Argentina, and may have been following a policy which is out of line with the new top-level decision. To get into line will be something of a task, and the Department's own intelligence organization may well have an important role.

The lowest level of departmental operations might be illustrated in, say, the Army Department's share in the detailed implementation of the top decision. Before it sends small-arms ammunition to Brazil to supplement the local supply it should know, among other things, how large a ground force the Brazilians plan to maintain. Knowledge of the Brazilian force in this situation would be what I have termed the intelligence of departmental operations.

213

5. DEPARTMENTS AND AGENCIES CONCERNED

In the two top ranges of "positive, foreign" and "security, foreign" intelligences, my designation of departments and agencies concerned is to all intents and purposes complete. In the other ranges of intelligence, which I note on the diagrams, my designations are intended to be purely illustrative. I have touched upon the more important organizations, but anyone familiar with the federal government could add many more.

6. MAIN CATEGORIES OF SUBJECT MATTER

These categories, too, are intended to be illustrative rather than exhaustive. Chapters 2, 3, and 4 treat in detail the substantive content of the kinds of intelligence which are the subject of this book.

7. A NOTE ON TECHNIQUES: THE "HOW ACCOMPLISHED" ELEMENT

All intelligence operations sketched out on the diagrams tend to develop their own special techniques for the accomplishment of their ends. These techniques are numerous and differ widely from each other—as widely, for example, as fingerprint and ballistics analyses differ from estimates of coal or wheat production. In a book of this sort there is no place for even attempting to list the techniques which are not peculiar to the "intelligence" under review (i.e. foreign positive intelligence). But one point must be made: Intelligence experts tend to consider the mass of individual techniques as belonging to one of two master categories, the *overt* and the *secret or clandestine*.

By "overt" I mean the technique of finding things out by open and above-board methods such as are used in all kinds of scientific, commercial, and journalistic pursuits. I mean the kind of technique you might employ if you wanted to make biscuits for the first time or ascertain the market price of a railroad stock. In some kinds of intelligence work, especially positive foreign intelligence, you can learn a great deal by these overt methods. You study the current published technical literature, or you read the foreign press, or you listen to the official broadcasts of foreign radio stations, or you walk down the streets of a foreign city (with no attempt to conceal your identity) and observe what is going on. Some intelligence devotees have said that you can find out by overt means some 90 or more per cent of what you must know. The remaining percentage constitutes the very thing that the other countries regard as secrets of state, and these things cannot be had without recourse to clandestine operations.

By "clandestine" I mean the technique of finding things out by various concealed, dissimulative, or surreptitious activities. I mean the use of such devices as wire-tapping, the undercover agent, interceptions of the other man's mail, and so on. Some branches of intelligence would get nowhere without using these covert techniques. The best example is, of course, the intelligence of counter-espionage, where the utter secrecy of the other man's spying must be more than matched by the secrecy of your own counter measures.

Since these two master categories of the techniques of intelligence may or may not apply to every branch of intelligence—depending upon factors of time, degree of emergency, and the official mandate within which the branch is permitted to work, I have not indicated a "how accomplished" element on the diagrams. The reader who wishes to think up for himself a clearly-defined problem in intelligence work will be able to make a good guess as to how much of either technique would be required to solve it.

The Branches of Intelligence of Particular Concern to This Study

Of the many kinds of intelligence activity described in the diagrams, only two are of particular concern to this study. They are the ones enclosed in dotted line on the positive intelligence chart, viz., *Positive Intelligence, Foreign, Long and Medium Range* (Overt and Clandestine.) This is the intelligence of high policy, national security, and the grand strategy: the intelligence required by our top-level foreign policy men in every federal department.

Is It Realistic to Imply That Each of the Many Branches of Intelligence Shown on the Diagrams has Its Own Separate Existence?

The outline presented above is highly simplified. Certain qualifications are now needed.

In the first place, it is not always wise to conceive too high a barrier between security and positive intelligence. There are phases of the one which are of the greatest importance to the other. Let me give an example. Suppose some foreign power set up an espionage system in this country to spy upon us. Pursuit of these spies is the job of the counterespionage branch of security intelligence and theoretically of no formal concern to positive intelligence whatever. To a certain degree this is the case. But there are byproducts from the counterespionage activity which are of highest concern to positive intelligence, so high in fact, that it has often been argued that security and positive intelligence (especially at the top levels of the foreign field) should not be separated at all. What are these byproducts?

Suppose that our counterespionage service moves clandestinely and penetrates the foreign espionage net. That

216

is, before it makes the final arrest, it insinuates one of its own undercover agents into the other man's spy net. Suppose he not only learns the identity of many of the foreign agents, but also achieves a position where he reads the communications and directives which the foreign agents get from their home office. These documents are not merely descriptive of that country's espionage activities; they are also likely to reveal a great deal about its general activities, policies, and plans. They may contain the very information which the positive intelligence people have wanted for a long time and which they could get from no other source. I should venture that the by-products of Canadian counterespionage in its uncovering of the Soviet espionage net in Canada were every bit as important as the destruction of the spy net itself. The Canadian positive intelligence must have learned things about Soviet policy which it could not have learned except by itself trying clandestinely to penetrate the Politburo—which task would have had its difficulties.

The moral of the above is that whereas, beyond all doubt, there is a kind of intelligence you can call security intelligence, and whereas a great many of the activities of this kind of intelligence are entirely self-contained, there are other and important aspects of security intelligence which pass over the artificial barrier I have erected and mix inextricably with positive intelligence.

So also with the theoretical foreign and domestic intelligence. For example, in the course of its daily business of recommending, making, and implementing our foreign policy, the Department of State encounters a large number of organizations of Americans whose parents came from foreign countries. Many of these organizations—the Poles for example—have strong views on what United States policy should be toward Poland. Now what these foreign nationalities in the United States think and do about our foreign policy is likely to be a matter of some importance to us, and the knowledge of what they think and do can be a very significant phase of what might be called *domestic* positive intelligence. But merely because these people are Americans by birth, and the issues which trouble them are American issues, there is no reason to think of them as an exclusively domestic intelligence source. The roots that they have in the old world, the contacts and communications they have with it, the old-world visitors they see and talk to, make them a subtle and sometimes a unique source of *foreign* positive intelligence. Here again, the by-products of a purely domestic intelligence operation may have a high significance for the foreign branches.

Sometimes domestic intelligence operations unexpectedly uncover matters of large concern to foreign intelligence. For example, the Securities and Exchange Commission sent an investigator to the Hawaiian Islands in 1938 to look into the unregistered sale of some Japanese government bonds. These bonds were being sold and bought by Americans of Japanese origin. Enforcement of a federal statute was at stake as far as domestic intelligence was concerned, but far more than that for foreign intelligence. For the investigation of the domestic issue revealed that the Japanese consul had curiosity about many things not within his legitimate jurisdiction, and had a large unofficial organization of volunteer agents reporting to him. These facts, and others, were matters for the urgent consideration of the foreign positive intelligence people.

Perhaps more artificial than either of the two preceding cases of arbitrary separation (the security from the positive, and the domestic from the foreign) is that of making too airtight a separation between what I have called the long-, the medium-, and the short-range intelligence. The separation is there, but it must not be thought of in absolute terms. For example, a new weapon may have been secretly developed and a few trial models put into a small military action. The existence of a few of these weapons may first come to the attention of the force against which they are being employed. Say that the weapon is a new fieldpiece, and the force it is being used against is a battalion of infantry. Intelligence of the weapon is of great operational importance to the battalion. The battalion intelligence officer must find out as much about it as possible so that his force will not be wiped out by it. What he embarks upon is the shortest of short-range intelligence activity; it could be properly termed combat intelligence. Yet what he discovers about the weapon may be of prodigious importance. If the weapon is effective, his short-range intelligence work is of significance not merely to the medium-, but also the long-range activities. A weapon like the German triple-purpose 88 mm. rifle, tried out on a battlefield of the Spanish Revolution, is a case in point. Knowledge of it was of importance, not merely to the Republican unit which first encountered it but to the grand strategists of all the general staffs of all the powers of the world. So, with the first guided missile, the first 50-caliber machine gun, the hedgehog, the V-1, and so on.

On the other hand, long- and medium-range intelligence frequently has its short-range importance. It is almost unavoidable that a thorough study of the long-term policy of, say, the French Communists—a study designed primarily to assist our top foreign economic policy people and planners—would not also have some small operational (short-range) value to one of our representatives in Paris.

Lastly, even overt and clandestine intelligence activities have a way of mingling with each other so that a hard-and-sharp line is sometimes difficult to draw. For example, when an undercover agent learns something through an activity for which his cover was not necessary—say, he read it in the paper—and reports it, he could be considered as engaging in overt intelligence. Or *per contra*, when an attaché with no official funds to spend for the purchase of confidential information buys a hungry and potential "source" a series of expensive meals out of his own pocket, he is pretty close to clandestine intelligence.

More important than this inadvertent merger of function is the inadvertent merger of what both overt and clandestine intelligence produce in the way of substance. An overt intelligence organization must have the produce of clandestine intelligence to make its descriptions, reports, and speculations complete. It cannot hope to acquire all that it needs through its own open methods; there will always be the missing pieces which the clandestine people must produce. But on the other hand, the clandestine people will not know what to look for unless they themselves use a great deal of intelligence which they or some other outfit has acquired overtly. Their identification of a suitable target, their hitting of it, their reporting of their hit—all these activities exist in an atmosphere of free and open intelligence. A good clandestine intelligence report may have a heavy ingredient of overt intelligence.

The real picture of the diversity in kinds of intelligence is the one I have been trying to block out in these last pages. Its essence lies in this truth: a very great many of the arbitrarily defined branches of intelligence are interdependent. Each may have its well-defined primary target which it makes its primary concern, but both the pursuit of this target and the by-products of pursuing it bring most of the independent branches into some sort of relationship with the others. Intelligence as an activity is at its best when this fact is realized and acted upon in good faith.

INDEX

6

STRATEGIC INTELLIGENCE
FOR AMERICAN WORLD POLICY.